I0571431

Guinea Pig for Brunch

My life as a missionary doctor in Ecuador

by

Andrea Gardiner

Grosvenor House
Publishing Limited

All rights reserved
Copyright © Andrea Gardiner, 2014

The right of Andrea Gardiner to be identified as the author of this
work has been asserted by her in accordance with Section 77
of the Copyright, Designs and Patents Act 1988

The book cover picture is copyright to Rachel Williamson

This book is published by
Grosvenor House Publishing Ltd
28-30 High Street, Guildford, Surrey, GU1 3EL.
www.grosvenorhousepublishing.co.uk

This book is sold subject to the conditions that it shall not, by way of
trade or otherwise, be lent, resold, hired out or otherwise circulated
without the author's or publisher's prior consent in any form of binding or
cover other than that in which it is published and
without a similar condition including this condition being imposed
on the subsequent purchaser.

A CIP record for this book
is available from the British Library

Some of the names in this book have been changed to protect
some individuals' identity

Scripture taken from the Holy Bible, NEW INTERNATIONAL
VERSION®. Copyright © 1973, 1978, 1984 by Biblica, Inc. All rights
reserved worldwide. Used by permission.

ISBN 978-1-78148-876-8

Praise for Andrea's Writing

"What I really loved was that through this book, we meet the people Andrea works with and helps, and the great way she has of drawing you in and making you feel as though you are a bystander to what is going on."

Wendy Sparkes, author

"It is not easy to put this book down... This is the fascinating, inspiring account of a true adventurer."

Jeff Lucas, Author, Speaker, Broadcaster

"Gardiner ... describes in lively prose the poor people in Ecuador she has served. She writes of becoming pregnant, marrying, adjusting to new motherhood, treating machete cuts and strange skin diseases, making hard adjustments to Ecuadorian culture, and finding grace despite her personal failures."

***Guinea Pig for Breakfast* in the TOP TEN self-published books in WORLD magazine, June 2013**

"It is an amazing book, which I would urge anyone with a heart for people to read... Once you start reading you will not want to put it down."

Woman Alive Book club Member

"What shines through is Andrea's determination to make a difference."

Life and Work Magazine, February 2013

Praise for Guinea Pig for Brunch

"*Guinea Pig for Brunch* delivers excellent insight into everyday living in Ecuador with the privations of poverty and danger laid alongside the simple faith and warmth of the individuals who come under Dr Andrea Gardiner's care. Woven throughout, Andrea honestly shares her own questions and struggles as she brings up her daughters in a culture very different to that of her birth. More than a missionary doctor story, this is rather an unfolding of one woman's journey of trust and obedience to the God who called her to serve the suffering. I heartily recommend **Guinea Pig for Brunch**, but beware – you will be challenged!"

Catherine Campbell, Author of *Under the Rainbow* and *God Knows Your Name*

This is a remarkable book about 'grace under pressure' and the miracle working power of God to change lives in the midst of crisis. It will stay with me for a long time...

Jen Rees Larcombe, Author

CONTENTS

ACKNOWLEDGMENTS

Thank you first of all to my family, who support us as a family and our work in Ecuador in too many ways to mention. You are each much appreciated.

Thank you to all who pray for and support the work of Project Ecuador. Without you none of this would be possible.

I am indebted to my first readers – Alison, Kathryn & Malcolm – for their helpful comments and critique.

Thanks to Rachel Williamson for allowing me to use her wonderful photograph on the cover and to Tabatha Design for the cover design.

A huge thank you to Vlady, Tamara and Emily for keeping me company on this crazy journey. Life would not be the same without you!

Last of all, I am so grateful to my Heavenly Father for the gift of each new day and His constant loving care. I am so glad nothing can separate me from His immense love.

PROLOGUE

When I was a child, I somehow got the impression God created us because He was lonely and needed some company. I imagined God had need of us. I thought I had the right to demand certain things of God. I thought it was normal to expect a long, healthy, pain-free life.

Perhaps this is why Doña Elvira's story broke my heart so easily. I had no armour to protect myself from her devastating reality. I had no way of making sense of her suffering.

Her lively nine-year-old son, Emilio, had just been trying to pick an orange off the tree, which grew tall and strong in their garden. It was something he had done a hundred times before. He would reach up with his bamboo cane to knock a ripe orange from a branch and then suck on its sweet, refreshing juice on a hot, humid afternoon. Children all over Ecuador were doing the same. No one ever thought that it might be dangerous.

Emilio had lots of friends. He was a kindly, fun-filled boy, who was always getting into mischief. He was his mother's only son, the doted-on youngest, in a family of five. On that fateful day, he was playing with his best pal, Jorge.

"Let's try and reach those really delicious oranges high up in that branch," cried Emilio, stretching towards the sky, a huge grin on his face. Jorge was giggling behind him ready to catch the oranges when they fell. The boys were having great fun. Suddenly, Emilio's wet bamboo cane touched the live electricity wire that passed through the branches of the tree. He was electrocuted instantly and fell to the ground utterly still. Jorge stood there in shock. Then, he began to shout.

"Help, somebody help!" But there was no one who knew first aid. There was no ambulance to call. There was only blind panic punctuated by cries of disbelief. Eventually, the neighbour managed to find them a friend with a car who drove them to the hospital, only to have Emilio certified dead.

Doña Elvira was beside herself with grief. She could not believe her only son was gone. He was just a young lad. He had his whole life ahead of him. She never expected he would go before she did. She sat by his open coffin during the two-day-long wake and would not be moved. Her daughters had to hold her back from throwing herself into the grave with her precious boy. She sat for months after his death, staring at his photograph. She would not wash, cook or work. She was devastated.

But she did not ask God why this had happened to her son. Her loss did not cause her to renounce her faith in a God of love. Baffled and perplexed, I wanted to find out why not.

Chapter 1

What is Normal?

"I can't believe I've been living in Ecuador for four years already," I commented to my Ecuadorian husband, Vladimir, one evening, as we relaxed in the hammock in our garden. "Time passes so quickly."

The stars twinkled overhead as we watched the fireflies flicker in the darkness and smelt the perfume of the tropical flowers. Even at this late hour, the humidity and heat had me sweating and it was a relief to be outside in the soft breeze.

"I know," Vladimir agreed, "Tamara is already one and walking around. Where did our baby go?"

Two years of marriage seemed to have flown by. Vladimir and I had grown to be a good team, caring for our daughter together. Yet I still felt alien and different in many daily circumstances. I acknowledged to myself that we had married very fast, without knowing each other very well. We were united in our desire to create a loving family for Tamara, but sometimes the mixture of Latin and Anglo-Saxon, tropical and temperate was hard. For my part I loved Ecuador: its beauty and its people had captured my heart. Even so, there were days that I was tired of the strangeness of living in a foreign land, of always having to make an effort to fit in, of never quite feeling I understood what those around me were thinking. There were moments I fantasised about jumping on the next aeroplane out of Quito and zooming home to Britain. My mind would fill with images of me taking Tamara to the park with my sister, and snowballing in the winter snow. Sometimes I wished she were not quite so Ecuadorian and knew my country and my family better.

"Tamara is so cute and lively and she's growing so fast," I mused aloud. "She is well and truly part of your family, the apple of your parents' eyes. She's so Ecuadorian, for all she is bilingual. I would have thought by now that I too would feel totally at home here, but there are still things that seem so alien to me."

"Do you mean eating guinea pig?" Vladimir joked in his usual fashion.

"I quite like guinea pig," I laughed. I looked at the gentle, generous man I had married and sighed. "People always treat me as different to them, and they always will. I'm the "gringa". I see things differently from you. I'll never get used to the poverty, the preventable accidents and the patients with advanced illnesses that I see all too often here. You've grown up with the hardship and privation."

"What is it exactly that you can't get used to?" Vladimir probed.

"Really, I think it's the way people just accept what happens to them." I paused to gather my thoughts for a moment. "Take Sonja for example. She had a baby just a few weeks before Tamara was born, but he died soon after birth from lung problems. When she spoke to me about it, she just said maybe it was for the best, that she already had enough children to look after and that having a sick child would've been difficult to cope with. I know they're poor. I don't know how they make ends meet, but they look after their other three children well. They certainly love them very much. Did Sonja really not mind that her baby died? How could she accept such a tragedy?"

"Of course Sonja was sad that her baby died. What she said to you was just her way of accepting what had happened. She mourned her lost son deeply," Vladimir explained.

"So why did she never ask why *her* son had to die?"

"She accepted it as her destiny. Her baby's dead and gone. No amount of questions is going to change that," Vladimir replied quietly.

"But maybe that baby could've been saved. Maybe his lung problem could've been treated had she been in a better hospital. His problem might have been curable. I'd bet you anything he would've survived had he been born in a British hospital. I think that's what frustrates me. So many illnesses for which there are remedies go untreated. So many accidents here could be prevented. Life seems so cheap to people, because of the way they just accept what happens to them," I remonstrated. "Maybe it's the lack of education. Folk have never learnt to question what they were taught. They lack the ability to rationalise, to apply scientific principles and theories. Maybe they don't realise accidents can be prevented and disasters averted."

"There may be truth in that, but prevention and treatment need resources, not just knowledge. Life isn't cheap to people, they fight tooth and nail to survive.

But, in the face of death we acknowledge ultimately that God gives and God takes away. Who are we to argue?"

I contemplated these ideas, trying to make sense of them that night, as we rocked in the hammock and smelled the heady perfume of the exotic flowers on the breeze. I appreciated the Ecuadorian people deeply. Many of my patients came to mind. They had been extremely brave and very accepting. I felt I had much to learn from them, but it was hard for me to see life from their perspective.

I came from a country where people assumed that they would live out their eighty years or more healthily and comfortably. I thought it was normal to expect to have more than enough food to eat in the cupboard, plenty of clothes in the wardrobe, a free education and a world-class health service at my disposal. Likewise, I took it for granted that God would provide me with good things and would protect me from harm. In a land where we strove to shield ourselves from every possible injury with our risk assessments, insurance policies and national health service, who would love a God who did any less for His children? In Ecuador, I was astounded to discover there were people who loved God no matter what.

* * *

I was introduced to Don Claudio during my first year in Ecuador. He was a gentle, softly spoken, unassuming man in his fifties. He lived in a wooden shack built on stilts with his wife and younger children. They were caretakers for a small farm. They lived there in exchange for providing security for the property while the rich owners lived in the city. My first impression was of a poor, humble family doing their best to survive from one day to the next.

These were exactly the kind of people I had gone to Ecuador to help. My first visit to Ecuador, at the tender age of eighteen, had left me with an indelible sense of privilege and indebtedness. The personal contact with children living in poverty had made me want to give something back. I had felt so rich, educated and advantaged in comparison. I had felt compelled to return as a fully-fledged doctor to do what I could to alleviate their suffering and redress some of the injustices. As a medic, I had gone expecting to be able to prevent tragedy and cure sickness. I expected God to do His part in making this ideal a reality.

The first time I went to visit Don Claudio's house was at the request of Tania, the penultimate daughter. Unlike her umpteen older brothers and sisters, Tania wished to go to secondary school. I went to ask her father if Tania could join the sewing group I ran so that she could earn enough to pay her own way through school.

As I approached the rickety house, a little girl ran up the steps and hid shyly inside, peeking through the cracks in the wall to gain a glimpse of the strange, white visitor. This was Tania's younger sister Lorena. A stunning young woman busied herself in the tumbledown kitchen preparing me a fresh guanabana fruit juice laced with several heaped spoonsful of sugar. I discovered she was Tania's next older sister and the beauty queen of the village. Tania, her delicate face framed in a cascade of perfectly formed, black ringlets, proudly presented me to her father and mother as we sat on a pair of wobbly, old wooden benches in the late afternoon sun, sipping the fruit juice and exchanging pleasantries. A few chickens scratched in the dust around us and the mosquitos buzzed searching for a tasty piece of flesh to land on. Slapping our legs at the annoyance, finally we came to the business in hand.

"Sir, I've come to ask you if you might let Tania join our sewing group," I began tentatively. "She tells me she finished primary school last year and has not been able to go to secondary school. I would like to offer her work through the sewing group so that she can pay for her bus fares, books and uniform and so be able to continue to study. What do you think of the idea?"

Tania's father, Don Claudio, looked at the ground thoughtfully, rubbing his chin. The kindly creases in his weather-beaten face were drawn up in concentration. We waited with baited breath for him to break the ensuing silence and pronounce his verdict. I could see that Tania was very excited at the idea she might be able to gain more of an education. She looked at her wiry, thin father in suspense.

Don Claudio was not sure that further education was necessary.

"Well now, I don't rightly know," he began slowly, pondering the notion. "I can see the point of a boy gaining an education so that he can learn a trade and support his family and bring up his children right. But girls just get married and look after the children. They need to know how to cook and wash and rear a few chickens in the yard. Look at my older daughters. Fredis married when she was fifteen. She has three strong children and her husband provides all they need. Or take Maria, she has two fine boys and lives with her mother-in-law who suffers with memory problems now.

She does a good job of looking after them all. What more would an education have done them?"

I could see Tania's face falling, as her hopes and dreams for a better future seemed to be drifting out of her reach. However, Don Claudio had not yet finished.

"Tania, on the other hand, does suffer from a sickness Doctor." Don Claudio looked at me confidingly. "She has fungal infections in her hands. She's had them for a long time now. She can't wash or cook very well because having her hands in water makes them worse. I do fear she may never have a husband. Perhaps she should study, in case she has to provide for herself one day."

As I looked at beautiful Tania, I could not for one moment imagine that she would remain unmarried. On the contrary, I rather hoped she would indeed manage to finish her education before being in the family way. Seeing her radiant face alight with aspirations and ambitions, I hastily turned to gracious Don Claudio.

"I want to thank you Sir, for giving Tania this opportunity," I stated, smiling. "I'm sure you won't regret it and that Tania will make you very proud of her."

"Oh I am proud of my daughters," Don Claudio affirmed. "I'm glad to make Tania happy."

I was so pleased to be able to help Tania achieve her dream of attending school. I had come to Ecuador to make this kind of difference in the lives of individuals. It fitted with my worldview that life should be happy, prosperous and long.

I was also very impressed with Don Claudio. He was such a content and serene man. His gentleness was a stark contrast to the usual "macho" men in Ecuador, who had to prove how tough they were all the time. His wife, daughters and granddaughters were all very fond of him. His neighbours spoke well of him. He seemed to live at peace with the world. I wondered if having low expectations of life was the key to his tranquillity, or if it was something deeper. I did not know then that his resilience was about to be tested to the utmost and along with it my expectations of life.

* * *

Tania was just beginning her first year of secondary school when Don Claudio developed difficulty in swallowing. At first he did not pay much heed, figuring it would go away of its own accord. He tried a few natural remedies in the hope that they would be sufficient to solve the problem. When the weeks past and he was getting worse, his family began to be worried and remarked upon it to their neighbours. One of their neighbours was Hortencia, a health promoter who worked with me in the village health centre, and she asked me about it. Concerned, I went with Hortencia to visit Don Claudio for the second time.

We sat again on the wobbly wooden benches outside the equally rickety house, accompanied by several of Don Claudio's daughters, and tried to find out how he was feeling. At first, he looked down at his dirty, unshod feet and was not very forthcoming. When Hortencia whispered in my ear, I realised he was worried that there might be a charge for my visit. Hastily, I reassured him on this point and he began answering my questions. A frightening picture developed in my mind.

"Don Claudio, it's very important you go to the hospital for tests," I insisted. I did not want to scare him, but knew I needed to impress upon them the urgency of the situation. "This difficulty swallowing you have has become quite severe, hasn't it? It might be the sign of a serious problem. You must be seen by a specialist quickly while it's still possible to treat your condition. If you don't go now, it might be too late."

"Yes, Don Claudio," Hortencia chimed in, "you must listen to the doctor. Tania, Maria, Fredis, you must make sure your father is attended to now, so that he can be treated and get better."

Everyone in the family looked worried. They loved their father and wanted to do the best for him that they could. Fredis and Maria rose to walk down the dirt path to the makeshift gate with us.

"We don't have much money doctor," the young women confided. "But our father has been so good to us; we want to do all we can to make sure he is well. We'll take him to the hospital next week."

I was glad to hear the family wanted to see him treated, because so many in his position opted not to pursue medical treatment. I remembered the woman in her forties who had refused conventional treatment for her uterine cancer because she had believed the man selling natural remedies, who had claimed his herbal syrup would cure her cancer. She had died three months later of a haemorrhage. Others simply could not find the money, or the people who would lend it to them. Often, they were too afraid. There were so many rumours and anecdotes circulated about the harm chemotherapy did, without the understanding of the good it could do. Patients were said to suffer terribly and die regardless. Most people did not know anyone who had survived a diagnosis of cancer.

Quiet Don Claudio proved to be courageous. Tests in the hospital revealed a malignant tumour in his oesophagus. He had cancer. Still in the prime of life and with young children to bring up - he had cancer. Poor and with no social security - he had cancer. Don Claudio had to decide whether he wanted to proceed with the costly surgery and radiotherapy the specialists told him he needed, in the hope of more years of life to be able to work and provide for his daughters. If the treatment failed, he would be leaving them with no breadwinner and huge debts. Neighbours and friends debated the value of treatment and told him horror stories about surgeries that had gone wrong. Some offered herbal medicines or snakes in alcohol as an alternative treatment. Others urged him to go to the witchdoctor.

His daughters all implored him to go ahead with the operation.

Neither Don Claudio, nor his family, once complained about this arrow that life had shot at them. His wife, a softly spoken, short, plump woman, was bemused by the chain of events, but was doing all she could to help her husband. His daughters put aside their own lives to assist their father.

The matter of fact way in which they faced the daunting unknown which was cancer treatment, spoke to me of their realism about life. I felt my mouth go dry and my hands shake as I spoke to the family about the diagnosis. Broaching the subject was hard for me, as I feared their reactions, imagining what I would be thinking in their shoes. Don Claudio knew that life was full of twists and turns and that it never promised to be easy. I was beginning to realise I was witnessing a humility that was sadly lacking in my own life.

Don Claudio had to find the inner resources to fight. It was all such a bewildering, strange and frightening experience for him. He had hardly ever been to the capital, let alone to the hospital. He was worried about how to get to Quito and how to find the hospital in the great metropolis. He was facing a huge operation to remove part of his oesophagus and stomach, which would leave him weak and dependent for some time to come. He was afraid he would never wake up from the anaesthetic. He did not really understand what the surgeon was going to do to him or how he would feel afterwards.

"One of the scariest things is seeing the other patients in the cancer hospital," Don Claudio confided to me one afternoon. "There are people there with horrible growths on their faces. Some have no hair. Others are groaning in pain. I don't want that to be me."

"You're fortunate your tumour has been caught early," I reassured him. "The doctors hope to be able to remove it completely. You'll have to take care of yourself after the operation, so that you heal up well. Just take a day at a time." I hoped against hope he would do well. I knew very few people diagnosed with oesophageal cancer were alive a year later.

A member of the family had to be with Don Claudio at all times while he was in hospital. The nurses needed someone they could ask to go and buy the next injection or drip fluid. They needed to be there to help him with his personal hygiene and to help him to start to eat again. It meant being miles from home in a strange place. It was a gruelling task, but they did it willingly, anxious to see their father well again.

The community rallied round too. Once Don Claudio had recovered from the operation, he faced many trips up the mountains to Quito for repeated doses of radiotherapy. He had to find the money for the bus fares and a hostel to stay in. He had no money left. He had already sold all he had and, unable to work, had no income. So the villagers organised a bingo afternoon to raise money to help him. Hortencia was one of the organisers, ever willing to help a neighbour in need. A group of them went door to door selling tickets and asking for prizes. The event was a success and Don Claudio was not only helped to be able to attend his appointments, but also heartened by the warm show of solidarity.

Tania came to visit me to bring me some of her sewing. She was doing some ribbon embroidery for the first time and wanted to check if she was doing it right.

"How are you doing, Tania?" I asked. "And how is your father?"

"I'm well, thanks be to God," she replied, "and my father is resting to recover from the therapies he's been having in Quito. He's finished the whole course now and he's very weak, but he's determined to get better so that he can get back to working on the farm."

"He's done very well," I encouraged her. "How is he in his spirits?"

"He feels bad that he can't provide for us at the moment. It's difficult you know. But God takes care of us and we're so thankful that our father is still with us."

"Did you have to pay for the operation?" I asked her.

"Yes, and then the radiotherapy treatment cost even more. We have a large debt in the hospital. They're letting us pay it off month by month for the next few years. But it's worth it to have my father alive. He's a very good father. He's always been so gentle with us.

He's not like my friends' fathers who beat them. He's always made sure we have food to eat and clothes to wear. I'm just so thankful God has spared him."

Soon, Don Claudio was making his way down the road from time to time to visit us in the health centre. I marvelled at his recovery and was worried he might soon show signs of a relapse. Thankfully, however, he recuperated well and continued his quiet life centred on his family. Tania continued to sew and study and make good progress. The family struggled to pay their debts month after unrelenting month, but I never heard them once complain. They chose to focus on the blessings they encountered each day. They gave thanks each morning for another day of simply being alive. They loved God in spite of their suffering. I watched their daily example with admiration and realised I had a lot to learn about the world.

Working as doctor in a poverty-stricken country, sickness, accidents and loss had suddenly become normal, everyday occurrences. To my surprise, people did not demand good things from God nor expect Him to shield them from harm. They loved God regardless. As I opened my mind and my heart to these new ways of thinking, I found myself on an incredible voyage of discovery about myself and about God Himself.

CHAPTER 2

FACING UP TO INJUSTICE

I grew up in England in a middle-class family and never wanted for anything. I enjoyed a happy, secure childhood, received a first-class education and was never seriously ill. I can only remember attending one funeral in all that time: that of a friend of my mother who died of leukaemia. No one in my family suffered tragedy that I knew of. I grew up expecting to live a long, happy life. I was confident I was in control of my destiny. I worked hard at my studies to become a doctor and pursued my goals. I was sure I would always have all I needed and more while I was able to work, and should illness or accident strike then the NHS, insurance and the Social Security System would take care of the crisis, protecting me from poverty and death. There was nothing that could touch me.

Despite being a Christian from a young age my daily preoccupations were very much of this world. Which delicious cake should I bake this weekend? Where should I go on holiday next? Which book should I read? I rarely spent time thinking about heaven or wanting to be there. Life on earth was good enough.

In Ecuador, my eyes were opened to a completely different reality. Life there was not the safe, predictable, controllable adventure that I had so far found it to be. The ingrained corruption and lack of organisation at all levels of bureaucracy meant nothing could be achieved quickly for love or money. Frustrations were the name of the game. When I walked down the bustling city street, I stood out as the white girl with the green eyes in a sea of darker skins, and the unwanted attention from the smarmy men made me feel vulnerable. The stern armed guards at the doors of the banks and restaurants made me feel afraid. Pickpockets and theft were common and I was constantly on my guard. Justice was a joke. Life and death seemed a lottery.

Fernanda was a young Mum whom I was visiting in the Orphaids charity orphanage in our village. Orphaids did excellent work looking after children who had been orphaned through AIDS, and a few of the children also had HIV. The dedicated community team did education in schools and churches, and visited and gave support to HIV-positive people and their families. The Orphaids staff had been helping Fernanda in the local hospital, until it became clear that she would be better cared for in the orphanage. Fernanda had three children under the age of eight years. She was suffering from AIDS. The first time I saw her in the orphanage, tears sprang to my eyes. She was emaciated. You could see her knobbly bones through her transparent skin. She had crater-like pressure sores from lying too long in one position, as she lacked the strength to turn herself. She also had fungal infections and parasites. She was weak; she barely had the strength to speak. I had to lower my ear to her deeply lined face to hear her whisper.

"Thank you for coming Doctor. Are you going to help me get better? I want to look after my children."

"Yes, I'm here to help you," I assured her, though my heart sank within me. "The people here will look after you well. You concentrate on getting well again." I sat for a while, holding her hand as her eyes closed and she gave into overwhelming tiredness. She looked like a feather waiting for the lightest breeze to blow her away.

* * *

Fernanda responded to the loving care she received in Orphaids, as a wilted flower revives with water. The orphanage was set in beautiful grounds in the rural village. The children lived in houses with their foster parents, and patients like Fernanda occupied flats made available for the sick. She was able to enjoy a comfortable, soft bed, private bathroom and freshly cooked food. The staff gave her medications to her regularly, did her dressings daily and sat with her encouraging her and sharing their faith. Each time I visited, I was delighted to find she was gaining ground, gaining weight and gaining strength. We treated her itchy fungal infections and the dreadful sores healed up slowly but surely. The foster mums in the orphanage delighted in making her nutritious soups. They had great patience in sitting by her and feeding them to her, spoonful by spoonful, as they would the little children they cared for. They sang hymns to her and read to her from the Bible, lifting her spirits and filling her with hope. I loved being part of a team who cared for this broken human being with such patience and dedication.

One Saturday, I popped in with toddler Tamara.

"Hello Luzcelly," I greeted the director of the orphanage. "How is the patient today?"

"She is feeling much better," Luzcelly was delighted. "Her family are visiting today and she's so happy. Those are her three little ones." I was happy to see that Fernanda could now sit up and her voice was stronger. The love and devotion in her eyes, as she watched her children playing on the floor around her, spoke volumes. Her husband sat stroking her hand, desperately hoping this improvement would be sustained. I took in the loving glance they exchanged, as they gazed together at their toddler, who, like Tamara, was just learning to kick a ball across the room.

"Thank you for all you are doing for Fernanda," he said as he warmly gripped my hand in both of his. "We're so grateful she's getting better at last. We just want her to be able to come home with us." Tears filled his eyes, as he looked at his wife and children. Fernanda's eyes never left her children. I lifted Tamara on to my lap protectively. She cuddled into my embrace with a smile on her lips, as she took it for granted her mummy would always be there.

"When is Fernanda's next hospital appointment?" I asked Luzcelly. The only way to get the antiretroviral treatment Fernanda so desperately needed was through the government programme. I was hoping she could be started on medication soon. Without treatment, she remained too vulnerable. The weeks of hard work could be wiped out in an instant.

"She has her appointment on Tuesday," Luzcelly informed me. "We're hopeful the doctor will agree to prescribe the antiretroviral medication for her. There was a shortage, but the new stock has arrived now, so there should be no reason not to start new patients.

She needs them so much to improve her defences. The smallest infection could carry her away."

"That's excellent news," I replied with a grin. "Let's hope they start the medicine as soon as possible." I walked home with Tamara in her pushchair through the flower-filled gardens of the orphanage, filled with optimism for Fernanda. She was such a young mother, who wanted to be able to care for her children again. I hoped she would be able to blossom and flourish like the abundant blooms around us. I hoped she would be able to regain her strength and return home.

When I returned the following week to check on Fernanda's progress, Luzcelly was furious.

"We took Fernanda to her appointment, but the doctor refused to give her the medicines." Luzcelly was really upset. "We told the outpatient doctor, that the inpatient doctor had said she needed to start on antiretroviral medication, in the hopes he would duly prescribe them. Unfortunately, it turns out the outpatient doctor sees the inpatient doctor as a rival, not a colleague, so he resents any suggestions that come from that source. He point-blank refused to prescribe. It's so unfair."

"That's awful!" I could feel the blood rushing to my head. "It's not as if you can even buy them elsewhere. They're the only doctors with access to these drugs. How can they be so cold hearted and withhold life-saving drugs? Now what will happen to poor Fernanda and her family?"

Luzcelly sighed, "There's nothing we can do about it, except care for her the best we can, and hope for a change of heart sometime."

I trudged home disheartened and worried about Fernanda. As I opened the gate to our house, I was greeted by Vladimir and our chubby toddler running up and down the garden.

"Tamara's very hot, why don't we take her to the river for a swim before teatime?" Vladimir suggested, taking in my tired look.

I loved the way Vladimir made time to spend with Tamara and to have fun with her.

"Yes," I agreed easily. "That sounds like a lovely idea. Give me five minutes to get ready and let's go." We set off together happily. These small adventures as a family were very precious to me. I had married Vladimir believing we would be very important to him, and was so glad it was proving to be the case. My optimism was restored. Surely the hospital doctor would see sense and prescribe the medicines for Fernanda soon.

* * *

A few days later, Luzcelly called me to see Fernanda.

"I just don't like the look of her," she complained. "She's developed a cough the past few days. Her husband brought her this cough medicine. Do you think it will do any good?"

I went in to see Fernanda, and turned pale, as I saw she looked quite grey and was lying down in bed again, her strength quickly sapped by this new attack on her resistance.

"How are you Fernanda?" I asked quietly, sitting on the edge of her bed and taking her bony hand in mine.

"This cough is bothering me," she whispered, her voice lacking strength again.

"Let me listen to your chest," I instructed, easing her forward. "There now, rest back. I'll give you an antibiotic to fight the infection you have."

As I left the room, Luzcelly hung back, and I heard her say, "Don't leave us Fernanda. It's not time to give up on us yet." I was taken aback, as I had every faith in the antibiotics I had prescribed.

It turned out Luzcelly's intuition was right. Fernanda died that night. My heart dropped into my stomach when I heard the news. I returned from writing the death certificate to regale Vladimir.

"There is no justice in the world!" I exclaimed in frustration. "How can doctors who have medicines that could have helped her, just stand by and do nothing?"

"Of course there's no justice in the world," Vladimir stated quietly. "Did you ever think there was? You only have to listen to the news to know that. Injustices happen every day to all kinds of people. Every day, people die before their time."

"They always say you could die any day," I acknowledged. "They say you might get run over by a bus or be diagnosed with cancer. But, in Britain, no one really believes it will happen to them. It hardly ever happens to your friend or neighbour. Here in Ecuador, you can't look away from it. You can't pretend it isn't possible. Here in Ecuador, these things happen to everyone."

"Yes, it's one thing to see awful things happening to strangers on the television, but it's different when it happens to our own friends, family and neighbours," Vladimir agreed.

"The Bible says, "Each man's life is but a breath."[1] We're here today and gone tomorrow. Life never felt

---

[1] Psalm 39 verse 5

like that to me in Britain. Here, life doesn't feel so safe and predicable. It seems very fragile."

"It's true," Vladimir took my hand in his. "While God grants us life and breath, we should make every moment count."

I smiled at him, and at little Tamara playing on the floor, and whispered a silent prayer of thanks for the blessings of family, love and health. I prayed they would not be taken from me. Yet I felt a disquiet that I should be so fortunate.

There were seven village schools in our area, some of which were quite remote and difficult to access, along unmade tracks winding up into the hillsides. The smallest schools had between twenty and forty pupils, with one teacher teaching all the children. The larger schools had up to ninety pupils, and three teachers sharing the load.

I visited the schools regularly for our charity Project Ecuador. We checked the vision of the children, so that we could provide those that needed them with spectacles. We gave toothpaste, toothbrushes and soap to each child every year, along with Bible storybooks. We did a Christmas appeal each year, to be able to give every child a gift. For many of them, this gift was the only one they received at Christmastime.

The school in Aquepi was one of the larger schools, with three teachers. The head teacher was rather a dour man, who struck terror into his class of older pupils. The other teachers were a husband and wife, Señor and Señora Velez, who taught the middle graders and infants respectively.

They were always very welcoming when we went to visit the school. They had lived in Aquepi for several years and knew the families well. When I had sponsors from the UK willing to help children buy their uniform and books so that they could attend school, I asked Señora Velez which families needed the help. She had tears in her eyes while she told me of families with six or seven children, living in bamboo shacks, who lived from hand to mouth. They were totally unable to buy their children pens, pencils, exercise books and shoes so that they could attend school. Sponsors made the dream of every child attending school a reality. Without schooling, these children were condemned to the same cycle of poverty as their parents. With an education, amazing opportunities were open to them.

When we arrived at the school with bags of toiletries, Señor and Señora Velez soon had the children lined up in the playground ready to listen to the hygiene talk and receive their colourful bags. The children responded really well to both teachers and it was obvious they had a good rapport with them.

"Boys and girls, I'm here today to give you a special gift. I hope you will like it and that it will help you," I announced. "Who can guess what's in the bags?"

Many wild suggestions filled the air, so I gave them some clues.

"They will help you keep clean and healthy. They will give you shiny white teeth. They will help you to eat with clean hands."

"Toothbrushes! Toothpaste! Soap!" The children shouted, waving their dirty hands in the air excitedly.

They eagerly received the brightly coloured bags and hastily examined the contents. I watched a little boy pull out the little Bible story, which was also in the bags, and start to read it aloud to his friend. The smiles on their grubby faces showed me how much they were enjoying this special treat. I hoped they would make good use of the utensils.

As the little four and five year olds returned to their classroom with Señora Velez, they chattered excitedly and rushed to show her what they had been given. She responded to their delight with wide smiles and many warm hugs. This was a teacher devoted to her pupils and wanting to give them much more than their ABCs. She knew their individual circumstances and their families, and listened patiently to their concerns, joys and worries on a daily basis.

The next Monday, I went to work at the health centre as usual, only to find Hortencia and Monserrat discussing an accident that had taken place the day before.

"Good morning Doctor," Hortencia greeted me. "We were just talking about the motorbike accident that happened down the road yesterday. Did you hear about it?"

"No," I replied, "there seem to be accidents every Sunday with the busy traffic. So many people come out to swim in the rivers and drive recklessly. What happened this time?"

"This time it was Señor and Señora Velez, the teachers from Aquepi School," Monserrat chimed in. My heart sank. They were such lovely people. I dreaded hearing what had happened to them.

"They'd been to town to do their shopping," Hortencia took up the tale. "Both Señor and Señora Velez were on their motorbike, and Señora Velez had their little baby in her arms. None of them had helmets on. They were coming past here just at twilight, as the dusk gathered. The sun set quickly as usual. A lorry had parked in the road without any lights on, probably before it was even dark. They didn't see the lorry and crashed straight into it. They were thrown from the motorbike on to the cement. Both of them died from their injuries. Only the baby survived somehow unscathed."

We looked at each other in silence for a moment. The finality of death hung in the air. Both devoted parents and teachers had been wiped out in an instant. A beautiful little girl had been left an orphan. She would not remember the parents who had loved her so much and had wanted to be the ones to care for her, cuddle her and teach her. It was such a tragedy.

"And what's happened to the baby?" I asked.

"The grandparents have taken her in," Hortencia replied sombrely. "She's all they have left."

Later on, I heard the lorry driver paid the family four thousand dollars so that the family would not press charges. Such was the value of two lives.

Señor and Señora Velez had set off to town that morning as they had done a thousand times before, never imagining that they would not return. Such was the transience of life.

The whole community attended the wake and the burial. The sense of loss was palpable. The little children in the local school mourned their beloved teachers, tears now mingling with the dirt on their cheeks. The little baby girl stared uncomprehending from her wailing grandmother's arms. Her parents were lowered into the joint grave, never to be seen again. The swiftness of their parting grabbed my attention. Without warning or premonition their time on this earth was up. Were they happy with what they had achieved in life? What dreams had they left unfulfilled? How would the aching gap they left in their family and community be filled? How would this affect their daughter?

I began to have an uncomfortable realisation that I too was not immune to tragedy. My belief that a safe, lengthy life was all but guaranteed, was shattered. I could no longer deceive myself that God would shield me from harm. Scouring the pages of the Bible, I realised that God had never made this promise. I asked myself if I could love this new God I was encountering?

CHAPTER 3

WHEN SUFFERING IS CLOSE TO HOME

Whenever we travelled from Santo Domingo to Quito we witnessed car accidents. The road was sixty miles long, and rose from three thousand feet above sea-level in Santo Domingo, to ten-thousand-feet altitude in Quito. It was a spectacular drive through the green Andes mountain range, with sheer drops and hairpin bends. Lorries and buses overtook on the bends in a heart stopping fashion, which all too often proved fatal. Accidents occurred every day.

When I had been young, free and single, I had not thought too much about making the journey whenever the occasion arose. Now that I was the mother of a beautiful little girl, I thought twice about it. I only went if I really thought it was an essential journey.

Vladimir had to make the journey much more frequently. We had bought a small farm and planted bananas and anthurium flowers. These were a heart-shaped bloom in a variety of colours, which lasted for two to three weeks in a flower arrangement. They grew in the tropical heat of Santo Domingo, but were sought after by the florists in the high altitude of Quito. Vladimir drove up to Quito once a fortnight to sell the flowers to the florists, leaving at five in the morning and returning late at night. Often he had to come down the mountain hairpin bends in dense fog, or torrential rain. Visibility could be non-existent and he had to negotiate the twisty road with hundred metre sheer drops along one side. Sometimes, he could not get down the mountain at all in the rainy season, as landslides on the road were common and blocked the road.

Month after month he returned without incident, until one May. On this occasion, he had gone away for a few days with his father as they had some tasks to do in the capital. I stayed at home with Tamara and awaited their safe return.

The house seemed strangely quiet without Vladimir's mischievous teasing and playful tickling. Entertaining a toddler by myself, I found time dragged without Vladimir to break up the day and chat to. We missed him.

Vladimir and his father decided to return late at night, instead of waiting until the morning light, and wasting another day. They were anxious to be home. I went to bed that evening thankful Vladimir would soon be back. I could not help worrying when he was away on these journeys.

In the morning, there was still no sign of him. Starting to worry about him, I phoned his mobile. The calls went straight to voicemail. I figured they must still be in the mountains where there was no signal. Maybe they had stopped to rest after all.

About two hours later, Vladimir finally answered my call and assured me he was nearly home. Something in his voice did not sound quite right, but he promised me he was fine.

"Don't go out anywhere this morning," he asked me. "I'm longing to see you and Tamara. I love you."

"Okay," I agreed, "we'll be here when you arrive. I hope you're here soon."

At about ten in the morning he finally turned up. But, instead of driving in the gate as usual, he hopped off a retrieval vehicle. Alarmed, I ran out of the door, full of questions but relieved to see that he was alright.

"What on earth happened?" I asked him.

"Let's go inside," Vladimir replied, putting one arm around me protectively and reaching for Tamara, who was in my arms. He took a seat, obviously very shaken. "I crashed the car," he began, tears escaping from his eyes. "I'm so sorry. It's really bad. I don't think they'll be able to repair it."

"I'm just glad you are not hurt," I reassured him, giving him a fierce hug. I had never seen him cry before. "What happened?"

"We were driving down the road, not far out of Quito really, when a lorry came at me on the wrong side of the road. There was nowhere to go to. One side of the road is a sheer drop. The other is a deep ditch, so I managed to drive into the ditch. The car flipped upside down. I don't know how none of us were hurt. My Dad and my Uncle were both with me in the car, but thankfully we all had our seatbelts on. The car's a mess. I don't know how we came out of it unscathed."

"Where's the car?" I asked.

"I had to hire a retrieval vehicle to bring it down the mountain. The police from the toll at the top of the mountain were soon on the scene, and they helped us out and called for the rescue truck. We had to make statements, but the lorry just drove off. We've no idea who it was. We rode back on the rescue truck, and we left the car in the yard of a friend who is near the insurance company in town. I'm so glad we at least have the car insured! Anyway we'll have to go there later and see what they say, but I doubt they will repair it."

When I saw the car later, a shudder ran down my spine. It was indeed severely bashed and buckled on all sides. It was impossible to open the doors and all the glass was smashed. I could only imagine the terror of the men involved as they rolled off the road. I closed my eyes in thankfulness that no harm had come to the passengers – this time.

"Oh Vladimir, I'm so glad you are all fine," I exclaimed, staring at the car, my eyes wide in horror. "You must be careful driving up and down that mountain. It's such a dangerous road. I wish you didn't do it so often. What will Tamara and I do if you don't come home one day?"

"I will," Vladimir tried to reassure me. "Thanks to God, we're fine. I'll always come home to you."

"Tamara adores her Papi," I shivered. "We don't want to lose you."

No matter how much Vladimir insisted he would be okay, I knew that he could not promise me that. The accident increased my fear that each trip Vladimir made might be his last.

My bubble had been burst. I could no longer ignore the fact that no matter how many precautions we take, no matter if we are rich or poor, no matter if we consider ourselves good or bad, the unexpected can and does happen.

When I first went to Ecuador, I was conscious that being a missionary in a foreign land did mean accepting a degree of risk. It was certainly not as safe as staying at home. However, I had assumed God would protect me and prevent anything too terrible from happening to me. Now events did not allow me the luxury of such delusions. Bad things happened to missionaries too.

***

I was relaxing at home one Saturday several months after the car accident. We now had a replacement pick-up truck. Vladimir was on his way home from doing some shopping in town and Tamara was pottering around the garden picking the brightly coloured flowers that she loved. A compatriot of mine phoned to say she had a medical problem.

"We have a team of young people here from Britain at the moment," she informed me. "They're building in a town an hour from here. I went to visit them and one of the lads isn't very well. He has asthma and the local doctor thinks he might be having an attack. I'm a bit worried about him so I'm bringing him to Santo Domingo. Would you mind having a look at him?"

"Of course," I replied. "Bring him to my house. I'll be in all day."

An hour later, just as Vladimir returned, they arrived at my house. Ben, a young man in his teens walked into our house with help from two of his friends. As soon as he sat down he appeared to fall asleep, slumping over to one side. However, when I talked to him he replied in a slurred voice. He was obviously still hearing and understanding what was going on around him.

While I asked questions to try to gain a better understanding of what had been going on and the treatment he had already had for this problem, Ben seemed to become progressively drowsier. One minute he was joking about how hungry he was and how a guinea pig would be preferable to a KFC, and the next he stopped talking altogether and slumped on to the floor. Then, to my horror, he stopped breathing while lying there on my living room floor. My heart leapt into my mouth. He couldn't die here, he just couldn't. He had come to help out. He had come to serve God. This could not be happening. God should protect him.

"Quick!" I shouted to Vladimir, breaking out in a sweat, "help me get him to the car. He's stopped breathing. We need to get him to a hospital as quick as we can!"

As fast as we could, we lifted Ben into the back of the pick-up truck. I frantically rubbed his sternum and spoke to him urgently.

"Stay with us Ben," I urged him. "Stay with us!"

Ben roused a little again and took a breath. Groggily he asked, "Where am I?" over and over again, until he sank once again into the unnatural sleep that threatened to take him from us.

I shouted to little Tamara, who was still playing in the garden, to run to our good friend Mary next door, while Vladimir started backing out of the gate. I desperately wondered if we would be able to get to help in time.

It was the longest twenty-minute drive of my life. I don't know how many times I repeated the sternal rubbing and talked and talked to Ben. I don't know how many times he repeated the same question, "Where am

I?" and how many times he just stopped taking breath. All that kept running through my head was, "We cannot lose him. He has to make it. Please, God, don't let him die."

I looked up wildly, as we came to the roundabout and stared towards the hospital… only to find it was all shut up. Vladimir shouted to a passer-by asking where it had moved to and got directions, simultaneously driving quickly to the next roundabout. Relief does not begin to describe my emotions as we finally made it with Ben still breathing to the front entrance.

Once inside the Emergency Department I explained the story to the doctor as quickly as I could. As the doctor put a pulse oximeter on Ben's finger to measure how much oxygen was in his blood, I was alarmed to see the percentage falling from the usual ninety-nine per cent down to ninety, then eighty, then seventy, then sixty. Suddenly, he started having a seizure.

"Hey, you need to do something!" I cried to the doctor, who hit Ben's sternum with some force and put on an oxygen mask.

After that they took over. They performed a head scan, did a lumbar puncture and took him up to intensive care on a respirator.

No one was allowed in with him to intensive care, so we sat outside waiting for news.

"Well, at least we got him this far," I commented to Vladimir, sighing with relief. "What an awful thing to happen! He's so far from home. His family are going to be frantic when they are contacted. What a nightmare to have your son half way round the world fighting for his life! You just don't expect that to happen when your healthy youngster sets off, all excited, on a trip, do you?"

"He's so young to get sick," Vladimir replied. "What on earth can be wrong with him?"

"Let's hope the doctors can find out and, more importantly, treat it. They don't have many resources here in Santo Domingo. He needs to be moved to Quito as soon as possible, in my opinion."

When it became obvious things were under control and there was nothing more we could do that afternoon for Ben, Vladimir and I set off for home, both subdued.

"I've lost my confidence in life," I mused. "It seems like calamities happen to the young and to the old, to Ecuadorians and to the British, all the time. I finally, really believe it could be *me* tomorrow."

"Well of course it could." Vladimir replied. "That's life isn't it? You never know what is going to happen tomorrow. But there's no point in worrying about it either. You just deal with it when it happens."

"I suppose I thought God would look after me," I admitted a little sheepishly.

"Well, He does doesn't He?" Vladimir replied somewhat bemused by my comment. "Every day we have is a gift from Him."

"Every day we have is a gift from God." I repeated, savouring the simple truth found in those words. "But in that case I wonder if I should be living in a dangerous country when I could be keeping safe in the UK?"

Chapter 4

Living in Fear

The next day the doctors were no closer to a diagnosis for Ben: theories ranged from him having been exposed to a hypnotic drug, to some form of encephalitis. They could not give him any specific treatment. The good thing was he seemed much improved. He was off the ventilator, awake and breathing for himself. His teammates decided to seize the opportunity to move him to a hospital in Quito.

While they were booking a private ambulance to make the journey, I was handed the phone to talk to Ben's mother who was calling from England. What do you say to a mother whose son is critically ill on the other side of the world? I could not even tell her a diagnosis. No one knew what was causing the problem. My heartbeat increased as I took the phone. I advised her to come to Ecuador. It was what I would do, were it my daughter in that situation. She was on the next flight.

To check Ben out of the hospital, the bill had to be paid. It was over a thousand dollars and had to be paid in cash, as for some reason the hospital did not accept credit cards on a Sunday. We each helped by taking out the cash we could from cash dispensers to pay the bill.

Ben was wheeled out to the ambulance on a stretcher. He looked bright and alert and was complaining in a loud voice, that was music to our ears.

"I am so hungry!" He exclaimed to his friends. "When are you going to get me something to eat? I could eat ten hamburgers right now!"

His friends smiled and laughed in response. Their huge relief was palpable. As they climbed into the back of the small ambulance with him, they chuckled, "Don't worry mate, we've got some supplies in our bag." The ambulance doors swung shut, the engine roared to life, and they were off up the mountain. Vladimir and I exchanged a gentle smile, as we watched them disappear from view. However, we did not stop praying for Ben's safety.

"I hope the hospital in Quito is better equipped to help him, and that he doesn't relapse on the way up the mountain," I worried aloud to Vladimir. "I know he looked good just then, but he hasn't had any treatment for the underlying cause of the problem yet. He could sink back into unconsciousness."

"They have to get him to Quito. They have much better specialists and equipment than they do here. I'm sure he can make the three-hour drive. He looked great just now." Vladimir was optimistic. "Anyway, us standing here worrying isn't going to help. Let's go and get something to eat. It's lunch-time already, and I'm hungry!"

I was happy to make the most of a lunch with my dear husband and little Tamara. My increasing awareness of the wonderful gift that is life, and its fragility, gave me a new appreciation of time and a lighter hold on my possessions. It crystallised in my mind and my heart what was really important to me; my family and the people who lived around us. I wanted to make the most of each beautiful moment that was presented to me.

I was learning to live one day at a time, appreciating each opportunity to make Tamara laugh. I was taking time to smell the flowers and to listen to the birds. Life was full of beauty. Each new day brought new patients to attend to, more children to help with their schooling, different ways to serve our neighbours. Life was fulfilling. However, each new day also brought new reminders of the dangers waiting to assail me. My life felt full of contradictions and uncertainties.

* * *

Tania popped in to see me one afternoon. She had some English homework she was struggling with and had come for some help.

"Doctor, can you explain these sentences to me?" she asked. "I don't understand how to put them into the past tense in English."

"Let's have a look," I replied, pushing Tamara on her swing in the garden at the same time. "Read me the first one."

Once we had finished the homework I gave her a glass of fresh guanabana juice, made from fruit on the farm, and asked after her father Don Claudio.

"He's doing well Doctor, thank you," Tania smiled. "He's keeping well, and working when he can find jobs. Of course, it's difficult to make ends meet some weeks. The cost of rice and sugar keeps going up. But we're just thankful our father is still with us."

I watched her go and wondered how they coped. I too found the rising prices were affecting what I could buy, and I was not trying to raise a family on ten dollars a day. I hoped Don Claudio would not have a recurrence. Thinking about him raised the phantom of my own fears of an early death.

It was a subject I could not ignore. I bumped into Ben's friend in town and asked after him.

"We made it to Quito fine and he was admitted to the hospital breathing normally. Then, a few hours later, he went unconscious and stopped breathing again. I'm so glad that didn't happen on the way up the mountain! He was moved into intensive care quickly. His Mum arrived the next day. It was such a relief to have her there and for her to take control of things. The insurance company arranged for him to be evacuated to the USA a couple of days later."

"Did they find out what's wrong with him?" I asked.

"No. They still didn't have a diagnosis. It all seems to be a real mystery. Anyway, he kept on getting better and he flew back to Britain on an ordinary flight. I think he's still in hospital there, but much better."

"I'm so relieved he is okay," I replied. "It was such a close shave."

"It's a profound relief to have him safely home," my friend agreed.

Despite being a doctor and seeing sick people on a daily basis, Ben's illness in a foreign land took me aback. Somehow the fact he was English, and younger than me, forced me to face my own mortality and look death in the face. I felt vulnerable, as I caught a glance through the curtain that separates this world from the next. Death filled my dreams and jerked me awake in a panic. I began starting each day wondering if it would be my last, if this was the day God would allow something bad to happen to me. Yet, I had everything still to live for.

That night, I took Vladimir's hand in mine and guided it to my abdomen.

"We're going to have another baby!" I announced full of joy and full of fear. I was so excited. I had longed for and prayed for another little baby to accompany Tamara. Yet I was fearful too. I worried I was deliberately putting myself and my tiny children at risk by continuing to live in Ecuador. Vladimir left his hand resting on me, covering and protecting the miniature new beginning inside. I wanted that moment to go on forever, as we marvelled in silence at the new life we had created.

The call of life was so strong that, despite my fears about impending disaster, I found myself full of hopes and dreams as I imagined Tamara playing with her brother or sister, the laughter (and squabbles) in the years to come. As I have five siblings, I could not imagine life without a brother or a sister. My siblings had been my lifeline on many occasions and I wanted to give the same gift to Tamara. In the euphoria of the miracle of new life, I tried to shut my mind to all thoughts of vulnerability and danger.

Nevertheless, Ecuador would not allow me to close my eyes to the reality of peril. The next day Vladimir came home with worrying news. It was the last thing I wanted to hear.

"There are thieves attacking in Santo Domingo and its surrounds at the moment," he warned me. "Sometimes they fake accidents to lure others to stop so that they can steal from them. Sometimes they shoot or beat people in the process. It's been on the news today. I also heard my aunt's place was broken into last night. The thieves took the fridge and gas cylinder from her little shop. Last week Edgar, the carpenter, had his machinery stolen. They poisoned the dogs so that they didn't bark. Even the little puppy my Mum gave them a few weeks ago died. If you notice anyone following you home, don't stop at our gate whatever you do. Drive on to my parents' house where there are people about. And don't ever stop and help at an accident. It might be a trap. I don't want anything to happen to you and Tamara and the new baby. Always keep the gate locked and never let a stranger in. Just say I'm not home and that they will have to return when I am."

I listened to him in dismay. Fear grew in my heart, clutching it with icy tentacles. I did not want to be restricted in my movements, but I did not want to put myself at risk either. I began to doubt I could raise my children in this crazy place.

There was another road accident. This time, it involved one of Vladimir's good friends from university. Carlos was driving home in the early hours of the morning and he must have dozed off at the wheel. He swerved off the road and hit a lorry driver, who was standing by the side of the road to urinate. He killed the lorry driver instantly. To add to the tragedy, a bus driver stopped as he had witnessed the accident. As he crossed the road to help, another car killed him.

Carlos was taken straight to jail. The law in Ecuador states that any driver who kills a pedestrian is culpable and a jail sentence is always given.

Vladimir went to visit Carlos in prison and came back dismayed. He was being kept in a single room with about thirty others and one open toilet. It was a grim place to be: dark, dirty and filled with obscene comments from the hard-core offenders who constantly rattled the gratings of the room above. Carlos was facing years. Unless he could pay off the family of the man he had killed, so that they dropped charges. Then he would be set free.

The deceased man, it turned out, had had three common-law wives, each with children. Carlos' family went to negotiate with them and agree terms. He had to pay eight thousand dollars to each of the three women to be set free.

Vladimir and his friends donated a pig and organised a lunch to help raise funds. Carlos' family gave all they could. Carlos paid the money about a month after his arrest and was set free. Such was Ecuadorian justice.

"If you ever hit a pedestrian, don't stop, whatever you do," Vladimir warned me.

"What do you mean?" I looked at him in shock. "I'm not a hit-and-run driver."

"You would end up in jail, and as you are British, the victim would ask for a huge sum of money to have you set free."

I gulped and turned pale. I absolutely could not imagine the horror of being separated from my little children. They needed their mummy, and I needed them. It would be my worst nightmare. Not to mention how I would ever survive in an Ecuadorian jail. I felt my chest constricting just thinking about it.

"If you ever have an accident, just drive off. Someone else will help them. Go into hiding and let us sort it out," Vladimir was serious.

I weakly sat down and shook my head at the way this conversation was going. What kind of bizarre place was this? Justice was non-existent. The illusion that I was in control of my destiny was shattered.

I felt overwhelmed by the insecurity and uncertainty of life. The perceived threats and dangers tightened the frozen fear-filled vice around my heart. Fear was a paralysing emotion, sapping my energy and creativity, encasing me in a prison of my own worries and anxieties.

I believed God was in control of everything. Even amidst the madness, confusion, pain and suffering, I believed God was present and I believed He had an ultimate plan for our good. But I knew He did not promise to protect us from all harm. I knew bad things could and did happen to good people, to people who loved Him.

I also knew I was putting myself in danger by my own volition. I did have the option of going back to the relative safety of Britain. I tormented myself debating whether staying in Ecuador was God's will or my own determination to make a difference in the world. I endlessly played over in my mind the question of whether I should be exposing my children to risks I could choose to avoid. Anxiety and indecision lurked at my heels, nipping me endlessly.

Vladimir was pragmatic about the dangers.

"I have lived here all my life and nothing terrible has ever happened to me," he assured me. "One time a lad threatened me with a knife on the school bus. I stuck my fingers out at him under my jacket and pretended I had a gun. He left. Another time, a thief stole my watch when we were on the bus to University. He got on and stole from everyone while waving a pistol in our faces. That was scary, but he just took our things and ran off. My Dad had his motorbike stolen last year. He parked it outside the fish market and when he came back with his fish, it had vanished. You just have to be careful not to put yourself in danger. Belongings are just objects. The important thing is that neither you nor Tamara is harmed."

"Don't you ever think we should go and live somewhere else?" I suggested weakly.

"This is my home. It's always been like this. I've never known anywhere else and there are plenty of places that are more dangerous. It's in places like this that the people need the help of the charity," he responded.

"Can you ever see yourself living in Britain?" I asked him.

"No," was the short reply. "I love visiting, but what would I do there? My degree is not recognised there. I couldn't earn much." Irrepressible, his sense of humour came to the fore. "Besides I would miss my food too much. How would I live without barbequed guinea pig and cow's stomach in peanut sauce?"

"Well, I'm very happy to be able to do the charity work," I agreed. "Every time a patient, who arrived despondent in a wheelchair, dances out the door a few months later, I cannot imagine doing anything more worthwhile. When I see timid children transformed into confident young people, through the opportunity to go to school, I'm so glad I'm here and able to help them. I just get scared sometimes. Things happen here that would *never* happen in Britain. There is such a lack of policing. There is no concept of health and safety. I feel vulnerable, a target, because I'm white. And yet, I would be loath to give up the amazing privilege of being able to help patients and send children to school. It's an amazing life we lead. I just never know what is around the next corner." I let out a deep sigh. "I wish I could feel secure. I wonder if I will ever be able to relax?"

CHAPTER 5

FACING THE FOE

While the dangers and uncertainties of life in Ecuador pushed me to abandon ship, the tears of the suffering called me to stay aboard. This daily tussle was sometimes won by fear and other times won by optimism. In the end it was the undeniable reality of evil that focused my mind and steeled my will to continue to fight in the battle.

I was sitting watching television one evening with Vladimir, stroking my rounded abdomen absent-mindedly. Tamara was already asleep for the night. There came a banging on the gate – unusual for the late hour. Vladimir went to find out who it was and came back with a friend of ours, who had brought with her a mother and her little six-year-old girl.

The six-year-old (we will call her Jenny) clung to her mother, hiding her frightened face in her mother's skirts. She was a pretty little girl with huge dark eyes and shiny, long black hair. I could imagine she loved playing with a doll and playing chase with her playmates. We all gave the customary greetings and then took a seat. I wondered what had brought them to our doorstep so late at night. I suspected it was nothing good. Our friend began to explain the problem in hushed tones.

"We didn't know where else to go," our friend began. "Jenny was raped today and she's in pain. Her Mum took her to a doctor, but they wouldn't even look at her or give her anything. The doctor said she has to go to the police. I arrived home in the afternoon and heard the awful news. Now it's night time, and we don't even have anything to give her for the pain. I thought of you and was sure you'd help us. Can you give Jenny some medicine?"

I sat there dumbstruck, my pulse racing. What kind of person would make this terrible assault on such a young girl? She was just an innocent child. I looked at her cowering beside her mother and my heart bled for her. How had this happened? Did they know who had done it? A thousand questions began to race through my mind. I took a deep breath, and tried to gather my thoughts and to consider how best to help Jenny.

"The doctor was right that you need to go to the police," I replied. "I can't examine her, because it may affect evidence needed to convict the person who did this. The police have the expert doctors to deal with these cases. She needs tests to be done to make sure she hasn't been given any infections. They have psychologists to help her too. This is a very serious crime. Why haven't you been to the police?" I addressed the question to the mother.

"Well the man that did it is family," she confessed, in a soft voice, avoiding my gaze, "and his mother is dying of cancer. It would kill her to have her son arrested."

To be honest, I struggled to comprehend her answer. I could not grasp that she knew who had done this and did not want to hold him accountable. But I did not know the first thing about her circumstances, what relationship she had with this man or his mother or the dynamics of her family. I did not even know if she was telling the truth. I did know I had to try to persuade her to report this matter for everyone's sake. I was also conscious Jenny was listening to our every word.

"But Madam, this man has done an awful, awful thing to your daughter," I responded. "He will do it again to another little girl if he's not stopped. He can't just get away with this. Your daughter needs proper medical treatment. How do you know he doesn't have a serious infection? It's your daughter who is the victim here. Your daughter needs to be protected from this man. She needs to know she is safe."

"Yes, this is a serious crime," Vladimir agreed. "You cannot remain silent. You must report this. This man is a danger to other little girls."

"The doctor is right," our friend chimed in. "We really should take her to the police." She started to cry, "I can't believe he's done this to poor little Jenny. What kind of man is he?"

We talked for some time, and in the end the mother agreed to go to the police. I had some pain-relief medicine in the house, so I measured it out and gave some to Jenny.

"Here, this will help with your pain," I gently reassured her, though I privately thought her emotional pain must be much greater than her physical pain, and not so easily treated. "This is a terrible thing that has happened to you Jenny, but you are going to be taken care of."

They took their leave and disappeared into the night. I could not sleep for thinking about Jenny and wondering if we really had persuaded them to go to the police. The next day I phoned our friend to make sure they had gone to the authorities as promised, and was relieved to hear that they had. I could only hope the perpetrator would be arrested and kept from harming other little girls in the same way. Knowing Ecuadorian justice, I knew it was very possible he would remain free.

I felt physically sick thinking about what had been done to that defenceless little girl, and at the wickedness of mankind. I wondered at God's patience with us. Why had He not brought the world to an end a long time ago? In His patience with us I saw His infinite grace at work, His longing that each of us would come to know His love and become part of His family. I believed that He delayed judgement still, waiting for more of us to accept His offer of salvation. It struck me anew what an amazing gift Jesus' death for us was, as the Innocent One took upon Himself all our evil.

"Surely God has every right to demand of us why we cause so much suffering in the world – instead I all too quickly blame God for allowing suffering," I commented to Vladimir.

"We certainly do a lot of stupid and foolish things," Vladimir agreed.

"Jesus' victory over death gives us the chance to join the battle against evil," I meditated. "That's what I want to spend my life doing. I want to be part of the solution to this world's suffering, not part of the problem."

***

Unfortunately, Jenny was not the only child to suffer at the hands of her own family. Erika was rescued by Orphaids and brought to the orphanage just a few days later. She had been knocked down by a vehicle and left severely brain damaged. She was one of many siblings, living in great poverty with several social problems, and had been terribly neglected. She arrived at the orphanage absolutely skin and bone, malnourished like a child one sees on the television during a famine in Africa. No one seemed to know how old she was, but it was estimated she was about eleven years old. Her sparse hair barely covered her head, and her large brown eyes were sunken into her skull. She had pressure sores on her back, and her legs were contracted up in a foetal position due to lack of use. She could not speak or move herself much, but when the other children put some music on for her she inclined her head to listen and smiled. Some part of the original Erika was still in that emaciated, forsaken body.

It was heart-breaking to see that pitiful little girl, now resting on the soft mattress in Orphaids. What months of neglect had she suffered? How had they let her go hungry and unfed? No one had thought to exercise her limbs or to move her in her bed to prevent the sores and contractures of her arms and legs. No one had wiped her brow or sung her a soothing song or talked to her when she felt afraid. No one had tried to understand anything she wanted to communicate. She had been totally abandoned and forgotten about. She was a precious child, totally dependent on others, needing love and care. She had been let down when she had needed help most.

We set to caring for her in every way we could. We made her thin, thin bones comfortable. Tamara gave her a little pillow to put between her knees. The children of the orphanage sang to her and played near her, filling her room with laughter. We dressed her sores and started to feed her. She began to gain some strength and was able to lift her head and look around a little. She took an interest in the people that came to wash her and to dress her and to move her stiffened legs and arms. She responded to the music and laughter. As I watched the scene around her bedside, I thought that this was the love that she should have enjoyed from the beginning. I was so glad that at least she found this loving care at the end, that she did not die alone.

I think all of us involved in caring for Erika found she touched our lives. In embracing her and her suffering, we tried to share her burden and lighten her load. In touching her, we touched Jesus who was with her all the time and brought her to us. Unfortunately, despite our best efforts, help came too late for Erika. She had no defences left to fight off the infection that mercilessly spread through her body, and she slipped away one evening.

"Erika's death is such a tragedy," I sighed to Vladimir the next day as the orphanage arranged the burial.

"Her accident was a tragedy, and the neglect that followed, but not her death," Vladimir disagreed gently. "She is happy now in heaven, restored and free from pain."

"I need that hope of heaven to keep me going now," I observed. "Life would be too depressing without the hope of eternal happiness. Eternity is just so long. I can't even imagine forever and ever. It puts the briefness of our lives and our troubles here into perspective. On earth, all things come to an end. In heaven, we will enjoy perfect love and happiness forever. Do you think Erika has forgotten all she suffered now?"

* * *

A few weeks after Erika's death, I was asked to go on a visit to a young disabled boy, who had been found tied up in his house. It proved to be another heart-breaking experience. I set off with the charity worker into the countryside. Hampered somewhat by my swelling abdomen, we had to walk a good distance from where we left the car to reach the house. The house was a rickety wooden construction on stilts, and we gingerly climbed up the loose wooden plank steps to the front door. No one answered our knocks or shouts. Going around the side of the house, there was a tiny window. Peering in until our eyes became accustomed to the darkness within, we could make out the young boy tied up in the gloom.

He was about ten years old and had cerebral palsy. He was tied up by both wrists to the bedposts, so that he could not flail about. The room just had the one tiny window. He was shut in the dark all day long. The room stank of urine. The mosquitoes buzzed around him, biting him mercilessly. He was utterly alone. There was no one to hear his cries and groans.

Eventually, the boy's mother came back from cutting bananas in the field behind the house. She invited us up onto the porch and brought the lad out.

"My poor lad has been severely mentally and physically disabled since birth," she told us. "I am alone and I have to leave him by himself to be able to go and get us food to eat."

"Why do you leave him tied up?" My companion enquired.

"I have to tie him up because otherwise he thrashes about and hurts himself," she protested. "He ends up covered in bruises."

I went up to the frightened boy slowly and bent down to examine him. He was still blinking from the bright sunlight. His eyes were sunken into his skull. He had wasted muscles and tight, contracted tendons. He was malnourished and had sores on his skin. His wrists were bleeding from where he had been tied up. His teeth were all rotten and he was afraid of us. He sat on the floor of the porch cowering in a corner, rocking to and fro and not wanting to be touched. My arms ached to be able to scoop him up and take him to some place where he could be well cared for. The burden he placed on his mother was too much for her. They were obviously both struggling to survive. Neither the wider family nor society had helped or provided for this precious young lad.

It turned out he did have some adult, able-bodied brothers, and so the charity, Life In Abundance, set about enlisting their help so that he did not have to spend time alone, tied up in that dark room. The charity helped him with trips to town for physiotherapy and dental treatment and gave practical help to the family so that they could care for him better. He had a wonderful smile that lit up his face when he was treated gently, and a deep belly shaking laugh. I hoped the changes brought into his young life would be lasting, and that his circumstances really could improve.

Visits like that one were mentally and emotionally draining. It was confronting pain and suffering without the screens, anaesthetics and euphemisms we camouflage them with in the West. Yet facing up to the foe made me more determined to stay in Ecuador and play my part in the higher battle of good against evil. It also made the joys of life all the more wonderful, and worth celebrating and appreciating. Each small act of goodness, each tiny innocent delight was a whisper of hope in my ear, an encouragement to believe that one day, good will triumph over evil.

It was amazing to be able to return home to embrace Tamara, who was now nearing her second birthday. Tamara would laugh and splash in her bubble-filled bath each evening. She came out smelling so fresh and delicious. I would tickle her as I sprinkled her with talc and dressed her in her pyjamas, and then Vladimir would chase her round the room to make her laugh out loud. We would light the barbeque of an evening and grill some delicious flavoursome pork ribs, and swing in the hammock listening to the night insects buzzing. Sometimes fireflies would dart and flicker past us, lighting up the darkness with their magical twinkle. Other evenings the moon would shine brightly, and the clouds would clear to reveal the myriad stars they had been hiding. Our home was my oasis, our family my source of refreshment and relaxation. They were part of all that was good and beautiful in life.

I gave thanks that Tamara and the little one kicking about in my womb were happy and healthy. I tried not to look too far into the future, not to worry about obstacles that were yet to come. I tried to accept the insecurity and misgivings that continued to plague me. I decided to focus on what being in Ecuador allowed me to contribute to the greater good. My journey started with learning to live in the present.

CHAPTER 6

LIVING IN THE PRESENT

The magical moments of life and hope were more plentiful than the traumas. My beautiful, much longed for Emily Megan was born one June morning. A sleepy little baby, she instantly stole my heart with her cute little face and warm touch. As she nuzzled in to nurse, I mused on the amazing miracle that each new life is. I wanted to protect her from all harm. I wanted to see her happy, joyful and laughing out loud. I took great delight in every cuddle. I savoured watching her learn to smile and then to laugh. How I enjoyed reading her stories and singing her songs, together with her big sister Tamara: Tamara who had taken one look at the new baby and said, "Wow!"

I marvelled in a toddler's ability to live so completely in the present. Tamara's innocent delight, expressed so freely moment by moment in her days full of discovery and fun, spoke to me of the need to leave the future in the future and to concentrate on the day I was actually living. I began to start each day with a prayer of thanks for the birth of a new day. While trying to minimise the dangers my daughters were exposed to, I refused to let fear for the future spoil the precious experiences of the present. I put my daughters into my Father's hands and trusted Him to help us through whatever lay ahead. I knew that the path may not be smooth, but realised worrying was not going to change a thing.

Emily was my constant companion. I carried her in the baby carrier down the road to the health centre each morning and she slept in the pram while I attended patients, waking every now and then for a feed. Sometimes her Auntie Sandy came and whisked her away to bounce her on her knee for a while, and sometimes her grandmother took her to look at the chickens and guinea pigs she kept. Emily was a very contented baby and took everything in her stride. At midday, we would walk back down the road to our house for lunch.

In the afternoons, I played in the garden with the girls or went to visit my good friend Mary next door. She kept me supplied with cups of tea, while I chased after Tamara. We enjoyed Emily's first smile, delighted in her first giggle and spent many hours with her asleep in our arms.

By the time bedtime came, I was exhausted and fell into a dreamless sleep, tired out but very happy.

The sewing group came to our house once a fortnight, to sell me the items they had made and for me to explain what they were to make next. These eight young ladies loved coming to jiggle Emily and play with Tamara while we discussed the new designs and looked at sewing magazines together. Tania made the most of her opportunity to sew and to study. She was a very conscientious member of the group. She had a talent for embroidery and learnt to do exquisite ribbon embroideries, delicate thread work and vibrant fabric painting. I gave her a sewing machine and she mastered that too. Soon, she was making elegant bags and fun pencil cases. Then she took on the challenge of learning to make clothes and produced gypsy skirts dancing with colour, and smart shorts for the boys. The group between them made three hundred skirts and pairs of shorts and I took them to give to the children in the local schools that year at Christmas. They gave so much joy and laughter. My heart brightened for months to come, every time I saw a child wearing an item we had made them. The children never forgot that Christmas.

Tania was doing well at school too. She carefully used her sewing money to pay for her bus fares, to buy equipment needed for science experiments and materials needed for art classes. She passed her end of year exams with flying colours and had no problems moving up to the next level.

Her shy little sister, Lorena, started coming with her to the sewing group. She had a very attractive gentle manner and her sister's eye for detail. She too was an excellent and keen student. Her father, Don Claudio, was helping her to start secondary school, as he was working again and his cancer remained in remission.

In the health centre, I never knew what was going to walk through the door next. I took it a day at a time, doing my best to meet each new challenge and problem. A girl came to see me, bringing her school report for her sponsor. She had asked her neighbour for a lift to the health centre. This somewhat unkempt lady was waiting outside ready to drive the girl home again, when she went pale and approached Hortencia to ask for a glass of water. Suddenly, she fell to the floor in a dead faint and started to shake all over.

"Doctor, doctor, come quickly, the lady's unwell," Hortencia called to me. I rushed to her aid and kept the woman safe until the fit passed. She then dozed for a few minutes before opening her dark eyes to see our startled faces all around her.

"You had a seizure," I told the lady. "Has that happened before?"

"Yes it's happened two or three times now," the lady admitted, shifting herself from side to side in embarrassment.

"Have you been to the hospital?" I asked.

"Yes, and they said I need tests done," the lady grudgingly revealed, as she sat up slowly, eyeing the escape route.

"And have you had them done?" I prompted.

"Not yet," she said with her face deadpan. "I'm alone with a nine-year-old daughter. I don't have anyone to leave her with while I go to hospital." She stood up shakily and started towards the door.

"But Señora, you should not be driving. What would happen if you had a seizure while you are at the wheel? You could kill yourself and someone else. You should get the tests done and get the treatment you need. You shouldn't be driving."

The lady murmured something unintelligible, telling me without words to mind my own business. In Ecuador there was no DVLA to inform. I had no power to stop her getting back in her car, and that was exactly what she did. I got the impression she actually already knew what was wrong, but did not want to undergo treatment.

Perhaps it all seemed too daunting for her. I never saw her again.

The next patient that day was Don Claudio. I was pleased to see him. He had not been to see us for a while. He greeted me in his usual respectful, gentle manner, before taking a seat.

"Hello, Don Claudio," I smiled. "It's really good to see you. How can I help you?"

"Doctor, I need help with these lumps," he announced. "I am covered in them and they hurt."

"Have you been to follow-up at the cancer hospital?" I enquired, concerned.

"I didn't go for a while because we're still paying the debt for the treatment I received, you know." He bowed his head for a moment trying to put his thoughts into words. "My daughters took me a few weeks ago and they took a sample from these lumps here, but they said there's nothing wrong."

He indicated some of the lumps near his neck, which had little scars from where the biopsies had been taken. Without the results I was really none the wiser, but I found it hard to believe that there was nothing to worry about.

All I could do was give him some tablets for the pain and utter a prayer for him and his family, his beautiful, gentle daughters and his grandchildren. As ever he impressed me with his warm-hearted thanks and his uncomplaining attitude. He went on his way with a smile, determined to make the most of the day he was living.

The next time Tania and Lorena came to the sewing group I asked after Don Claudio, somewhat nervously, and was surprised when they announced he was much better and that the lumps had disappeared. The girls chattered about their school life and asked for help with their English homework. Tania had to prepare a song to sing to her classmates in English. I found a CD of Tamara's and chose a simple nursery rhyme she could learn. We had a giggle over Tania's pronunciation as she gamely had a go at singing the song. Tamara joined in, earnestly trying to show her how to do it.

"It is shameful a two-year-old can sing this song better than I can," Tania joked.

"Don't be silly, you don't have an English-speaking Mum!" I reminded her.

"Thanks for the help. I'll practice with the CD at home until I get it perfect for school," Tania promised. "Thank you Tamara for your help." She smiled at the little girl.

They returned home to Don Claudio and their daily lives, believing he was better again and that the lumps had been a false alarm.

Vladimir decided we should have a day trip to the beach now that Emily was a little bigger. "Let's have a day out and relax," he suggested. "We should take time to rest. I would love to eat some shellfish. How about some prawns in chilli sauce? Delicious!"

"Let's go!" I replied, remembering my resolution to live in the present, and thinking it would be wonderful for us to have a day together. So we went. We strapped the girls in their seats, put the buckets and spades in the pick-up truck and drove the two hours to the beach.

It was amazing to feel the salt breeze on our cheeks and to see the pelicans flying overhead. The crashing waves were the soundtrack to our day and the warm sun our companion. Tamara loved jumping in the warm surf on the beach and building sandcastles. She had a wonderful time. Emily was quietly content, and I was happy to relax in a deckchair in the fresh air.

Vladimir was soon hungry and ordered shellfish for breakfast. A buxom, dark woman at a mobile stall on the beach expertly sliced an onion so thinly you could see through the slices. Her thick curls bobbed and jiggled, as she next chopped up a tomato.

"You must take out all the pips," she advised us, "or the men end up with prostate problems." Scooping the onion and tomato into a dish with the shellfish, she proceeded to douse the mixture in lime juice. Vladimir added squirts of mustard and tomato sauce, and hey presto his breakfast was ready. It still looked all too alive and wriggly for me.

A few hours later, we enjoyed prawns and fresh fish for lunch. My favourite was the fresh melon juice with a hint of vanilla, and Tamara wolfed down the fried bananas.

We had our fill of splashing in the warm sea, and then wandered along the stalls on the seafront admiring the jewellery and the ornaments made from shells. We stopped in a bamboo bar to sit on the swings, and I had a fruit juice while Vladimir and Tamara sucked on ice creams. Tamara chattered away, enjoying every minute of her day.

Tired and content, we headed back home as the afternoon drew to a close.

"I'm so glad we went," I smiled at Vladimir. "We all had such a good day."

"We did, didn't we?" Vladimir agreed. He grinned seeing the girls were already asleep in the back of the car. "We mustn't leave it so long until we go again."

It was good to enjoy the pleasant things of life while we could. We arrived home very thankful for a special day with our dear children and beautiful memories.

* * *

It must have been a few months later that Don Claudio came to the health centre again as the lumps in his skin had reappeared.

"I've come for some more of those tablets you gave me last time," he requested. "They worked wonders."

"Of course I'll give you some more tablets," I responded. "But they're only for pain and inflammation. I think you'd be wise to go to the hospital again and get checked out."

"I don't think that will be necessary, Doctor," he disagreed. "They didn't do anything for me last time."

"That may be so, but I think it's time for a check-up by the specialists anyway," I insisted. "I'm worried about you."

"Well, Doctor, if you insist. Thank you for the tablets. I'm sure these will soon have me fighting fit again. Goodbye. May God repay you."

He walked out of the door and homewards. I had a sinking feeling that all was not well.

It was only a couple of weeks later that Don Claudio developed difficulty breathing. His daughters took him to the hospital up the mountain road in Quito as an emergency. There he was diagnosed with widespread tumour regrowth and given days to live. His daughters organised a private ambulance to bring him home to die with his family by his side.

When I went to visit, I was shocked by the change in Don Claudio. In the space of a few weeks, he had gone from the smiley man who had walked into my consulting room, to an unconscious man struggling to breathe. Tania and Lorena stood by his bedside, pain evident in their eyes.

I set up the oxygen concentrator I was lending them from Orphaids, and we gently attached it to the oxygen mask on Don Claudio's now flaccid face. His wife stood at the end of the bed wringing her hands, tears in her eyes. Five of her daughters were gathered there with her. They exchanged anxious glances and fiddled with bits and pieces beside the bed. I took them all to one side to encourage them.

"I'm sorry that Don Claudio is now so ill," I began. "It's hard to see him like this, isn't it?"

"Is there any chance he might get better?" His daughter Fredis asked, hope wavering in her eyes. I knew it would be a miracle if Don Claudio improved now. He was already very far gone.

"Our lives are in God's hands," I observed. "I think it is now God's time for Don Claudio to go to be with Him. The important thing is that you are with him at this time and caring for him. There are lots of things you can do to make him comfortable and keep him from suffering. The most important thing of all is that you are with him. Speak to him. He can probably still hear you. Hold his hand. Keep him company, until his time comes. Make the most of these last days you have with him."

"Oh yes, his eyes flicker when I talk to him. I'm sure he can hear me," Tania confirmed. "How can we care for him?"

As I explained how to wash him, clean his mouth and keep it moist, move him in the bed and care for his skin, the daughters paid close attention, anxious to do all they could for the father who had done all he could for them. They also had to learn how to administer injected medicines for his pain and how the oxygen machine worked. There were no nurses who would be popping in to help. It was down to them.

It was only two days later that they called me to write the death certificate. He had died in the early hours of the morning. I left Tamara and Emily with Vladimir and drove down the road to visit the family. Don Claudio was already being laid out, ready for the wake. The family left me alone with the cold body, the now absent heart-beat and fixed, staring eyes. In the silence and loneliness of that moment I paused to stop and stare, wonder and worship. The mystery that surrounded death nudged me closer to the mystery that is God. It reminded me again of the fleeting nature of our days. It filled me with awe for the God who creates and takes away. It lifted my eyes to a reality hidden behind the clouds, filled with thousands who have gone before. It put to shame my preoccupation with material things, and beckoned me towards heavenly qualities of kindness, forgiveness and love.

I said my goodbyes to the now absent Don Claudio in the silence, and thanked him for the lessons he had taught me. His great respect for his Maker, and acceptance of His will, had shown me my own pride and self-importance. He had taught me the lesson of humility. Like so many of his compatriots, Don Claudio said with the Psalmist, "What is man that you are mindful of him, the son of man that you care for him?"[2]

---

[2] Psalm 8 Verse 4

I had made the mistake of thinking that I was somehow better than or more important than other people, so if I were to suffer I had the right to complain, demand healing or expect a miracle. Don Claudio was just as precious a person as I am. He chose to trust God through his illness and into the next world. When things went wrong for me, I used to ask the question, "Why me?" I now thought the question should be, "Why not me?"

As I drove home to my family, my mind was filled with thoughts of the finality of death and the sense of loss a dear one's parting left behind. Arriving at the house, I opened my car door to be greeted by a lively two-year-old tugging on my T-shirt. Tamara was full of life.

"Come and jump on the trampoline with me!" She cried, excited to have her Mummy back. And so I found myself laughing and leaping and singing silly songs. It was the way of things. Even in the shadow of death, life goes on and is for living, enjoying and rejoicing in, while we have the opportunity.

Lorena came to the next sewing group. She was still so young, just starting out in life, and now she had to do it without a father. I was pleased to have some good news for her, a gift of hope to help her look to the future.

"Lorena," I called her attention. "I know it's going to be difficult for you to keep going to school, now that you don't have your father to help you. I've found a sponsor for you to help you with the cost of going to school."

Lorena stared at me with tears in her eyes and then a wonderful smile lit up her face with amazement.

"You are an *angel*!" She exclaimed impetuously, giving me a hug and a kiss.

"You are very welcome," I responded warmly, returning her embrace. "It's an honour to be able to help you. I know you are a good student and I'm sure you will do well."

I was no angel. Being able to help out a fellow human-being in these ways was simply an expression of my gratitude for the many blessings I enjoyed in my life. It was my contribution to the battle against evil. It was what kept me living in a foreign land and helped me to resign myself to the frustrations and dangers that were involved. It was choosing to be with those in need.

CHAPTER 7

THE GIFT OF GOD'S PRESENCE

As I reflected on Don Claudio's life, illness and death, I realised that the greatest gift I had given him was my presence with him in his times of need. I could not ultimately prevent his passing. However, I had been with him and his family as they walked through the valley of the shadow of death. God does not promise to keep us from all harm. He does promise to be with us no matter what. His presence is perhaps the greatest gift He gives us and one I was determined to share with others in their times of need.

Señora Muñoz and her family were an absolute delight to visit. The first time they called, they were unsure if we would be able to help them. Señora Muñoz had been discharged from the cancer hospital in Quito with a terminal prognosis and no further treatment possible. They were looking for someone to help control her bleeding, swelling and pain. Hortencia and I went along to meet the family. Making our way through a sea of mud, which was the unmade road that led to their house, we managed to arrive at her front door and were ushered up the narrow, winding stairs to their second floor flat. Señora Muñoz was seated on the sofa, worried about her health. Her daughter was hospitality itself, making sure we were comfortable, had something to drink and biscuits to eat. Her granddaughter was interested to know all about us, where we were from and if she could practice her English on me.

"My dear Doctor," her daughter began. "My mother had an operation for cancer about five years ago. She recovered well and was back to normal for a long time afterwards. She returned to her farm and looked after her chickens and picked her bananas. But then, six months ago, she started bleeding again and her stomach got all swollen up. We took her back to the hospital hoping they would be able to give her more treatment, but they just sent her home again saying there was nothing more they could do. A neighbour told me about you, dear Doctor. She told us you can help us. My mother is very uncomfortable and can't leave the house. She would like to feel well enough to do some housework and maybe even manage a visit to her farm. She misses her chickens terribly and feels so useless just sitting around all day."

"Well, I'm sure we'll be able to do something to help," I replied. "Now, you must know I can't treat cancer. Only the doctors in the hospitals do that. What I can do is give you medicines to take away the pain and swelling, so that your mother feels more comfortable and can do some of the things she enjoys again."

The daughter and granddaughter were obviously extremely fond of Señora Muñoz, and wanted to see her feeling better and smiling again. They looked at us anxiously, hoping against hope that we would be able to help them.

I sat down on the sofa next to Señora Muñoz and asked her what she was feeling.

"Oh Doctor, I'm just so sore around my middle and so swollen in my legs that I can't move. I like to be able to wash the dishes and cook some soup. I don't like to be stuck on this sofa all day. My daughter looks after me wonderfully, but I just like to be able to do some things myself."

The medicines I gave her worked very well in relieving a good part of her discomfort. The swelling in her legs and abdomen decreased and she was able to walk around more easily again. The next time we visited, Señora Muñoz was washing the dishes.

Hortencia visited to give her massages and encouraging chats, able to give her company sometimes when her family were out working and studying. Hortencia was such a gentle soul. She had a quiet, but solid Catholic faith and a heart brimming with generosity. She was always willing to go the extra mile. She encouraged Señora Muñoz no end, lifting her spirits and making her smile. The gift of her presence let Señora Muñoz know she was not alone.

Sometimes, I took Tamara and Emily with me when we visited and the family all enjoyed showing the girls their cat. One afternoon, they gave Hortencia a puppy. Tamara was fascinated, and began to ask for a puppy of her own.

One day, I asked Señora Muñoz if she would like a visit from a Pastor.

"Do you know I would love that," she reflected. "I used to go to the Seventh Day Adventist Church round the corner from me. Since I've been ill, I've not been able to go. I do have my Bible here and I love to read it, but my eyes are not as good as they used to be and it's a bit of a struggle to read the words."

I picked up her Bible and turned to Psalm 121. "I lift up my eyes to the hills – where does my help come from? My help comes from the Lord, the Maker of heaven and earth."[3] I read.

"They are beautiful words Doctor," Señora Muñoz declared. "Isn't it amazing that He who made everything, is willing to help such an insignificant person as me?"

Pastor William came along one afternoon to visit Señora Muñoz, guitar in tow. He had a very warm manner with people and the whole family received him with their inimitable hospitality and welcome. Señora Muñoz was anxious to ask him about his faith, as she was contemplating hers in the light of her illness. They found much common ground. Pastor William read to her from Psalm 31. "I trust in you, O Lord; I say, "You are my God." My times are in your hands."[4]

"God is here, God is here, as certain as the air I am breathing, as certain as the wind that blows, God is here." Pastor William sang softly, as we all joined in. It was very simple, and also very profound. Señora Muñoz found much comfort and strength in the Scriptures and songs, and company, all of which reminded her of the important truth: God was with her.

After Pastor William prayed for the whole family, he took his leave, while they urged him to visit again.

"Do make sure you offer such visits from the Pastor to other patients, dear Doctor," they exhorted me after he had gone. "It's a wonderful source of strength."

---

[3] Psalm 121 verses 1&2
[4] Psalm 31 verses 14 & 15a

Soon Señora Muñoz felt well enough to go to her farm for a visit. She stayed for a week and loved every moment. It was wonderful to see a dream come true for her, even at this stage of her life. She came back from the visit invigorated and enthusiastic; we all rejoiced to see her looking so well and full of life.

Grismelda was brought to see us in the health centre by friends of hers who were regular patients of mine. She was forty two years old and had been diagnosed with breast cancer three years previously. She had had a mastectomy and repeated doses of chemotherapy and radiotherapy and was now coming to the end of the road. She was such a brave woman, always very positive and determined to live every day she had to the full. Her husband watched her in wonder and some helplessness as there was less and less he could do to help her. She spoke of her two adult sons with pride.

"The problem is this ulcer under my arm," she began. "My friends told me you cured their leg ulcers and I've come so that you can treat my ulcer too."

"What treatment have you had so far?" I enquired, as I looked at the two centimetre wide hole under her right arm, next to her mastectomy scar. It was a tumour.

"The hospital is giving me morphine for the pain, but they don't put anything on the ulcer. The nurse took one look at it and said, "Oh my goodness, that's awful!" Her face, doctor, was one of horror. I felt terrible. I have faith that you can help me with it, because my friends have spoken so highly of you. After God, I am putting my trust in you."

"Your friends had ulcers because of diabetes. Your ulcer is because of the tumour. They are very different to treat. I can help, but I can't promise it's going to go away." I looked at her kindly to see if she understood. I was not at all sure I was going to be able to live up to her expectations.

"I just want you to do what you can. I have great faith in you. It's so smelly and sticky and weeps watery, blood-stained liquid all the time. I hate it."

Hortencia, with her ever gentle hands and great kindness, washed the ulcer and removed all the debris. We had to help Grismelda to hold her arm up as it was very swollen and heavy. With her prematurely grey hair and pain-lined face she looked much older than her forty-two years. Nevertheless, her brilliant smile shone through as she chatted and joked while we worked.

Tamara was being looked after by her grandmother next door, but she wandered into the health centre at that moment curious to see what was going on.

"Is that your daughter?" Grismelda asked me. "She's very like you."

"Is the lady sore?" Tamara asked me in English.

"Oh does she speak English as well as Spanish?" Grismelda cried. "How amazing!"

"Children just pick up what they hear. They're like sponges at this age. I always speak to her in English, and her Papi in Spanish, so she speaks both languages well." I turned to Tamara. "Yes, the lady isn't very well. We're helping her."

Tamara nodded sagely and toddled off back to her grandmother. No one minded her popping in from time to time.

Once the wound was dressed with a powder to stop the bad odour and a dressing to stop the leaking fluid, Grismelda thanked us profusely. Her friends helped her to their car to take her home again. She even limped out of the door with a determined step. This was a formidable woman. We felt privileged to be able to accompany her on this part of her journey.

Señora Muñoz and her family never took our visits for granted. They always prepared when they knew we were coming and had a drink and a snack ready for us. On arrival, Hortencia and I were ushered to the sofa to sip a coke and eat a sweet bread roll.

"How are you, dear doctor?" Señora Muñoz daughter asked. "How has your week been?"

"Very well, thank you," I replied. "I've been busy as usual."

"And how are your girls? Why didn't you bring them with you today?"

"Oh they're full of beans thank you. They stayed with their grandmother today. I've a few other jobs to do in town, which would be difficult to do with the girls in tow."

"And how are you, dear Hortencia? How is your granddaughter? You said she had a cold last week?"

"She's much better thank you. She's having fun playing with our new puppy. The pair of them wreak havoc with my flowers in the garden."

Only after we had drunk up and finished our rolls were we allowed to start asking about Señora Muñoz and her health.

"How are you today, Señora Muñoz?" I asked.

"I've been bothered with bleeding this week," she admitted sadly. "Is there anything you can do to control it?"

"There are some tablets that can help with that, but they are not available in Ecuador. I'll see if I can get some sent from Britain for you." I examined her and saw that she was becoming anaemic. "I'll give you some iron tablets now, so that you don't feel so tired."

"Do see if you can get the tablets," she beseeched me. "The bleeding is so draining."

"I'll do everything possible," I promised.

The postal service to Ecuador was not the best. Parcels could take months to come. Fortunately, on this occasion a friend was coming out to Ecuador, so she brought the tablets with her. Señora Muñoz was delighted. She took the tablets with great faith and was very happy with the results.

"Oh doctor," she cried, "I'm so much better. It's wonderful not to have that bleeding any more. I feel a new woman."

I returned home satisfied, though tired. We did live busy lives. Vladimir worked from the crack of dawn until evening, building and developing the farm, when he was not tending the flowers. I was glad he was busy and had created work in Santo Domingo, as jobs were hard to come by. I was so tired out by the time evening came, I fell asleep soon after the girls did. Time together was at a premium. Sometimes communication between us was lacking.

Sometimes making visits to patients was difficult, because Vladimir and I shared a car. One Friday, I had scheduled a visit to Señora Muñoz at two in the afternoon. At half past three Hortencia and I were still entertaining the girls in my garden, waiting for Vladimir to come back with the car. He had been held up in town buying materials he needed for the farm. By the time he did manage to get home, it was starting to rain. Hortencia and I decided to go ahead with the visit anyway. We knew that Señora Muñoz was looking forward to us coming very much.

That afternoon the rains were so bad that the roads in Señora Muñoz's neighbourhood were awash with mud and Hortencia and I had to leave the car a long way from the house and walk, the girls in our arms. Tamara was now approaching her third birthday, and was heavy to carry. In the confusion of streets being dug up and the rivers of water running down the roads, I became quite lost, and we had to phone the family to ask them to come and direct us to the house. The granddaughter soon found us and graciously led us to the door, laughing with us at our misadventure. We arrived hot, sweaty and mud-splattered. Mindful of the conditions we had had to endure to get to them, they had cooked chicken and chips to welcome us. We were very grateful for the chance to dry off and refresh ourselves after the stressful walk. Tamara and Emily received many cuddles from these ladies and lapped up all the attention they were given. We were made to feel we were part of the family.

Señora Muñoz's health was now deteriorating. She was no longer sitting on the sofa, but confined to bed. Hortencia sat and gently massaged her legs, while I asked about her pain, bleeding and swelling and adjusted her medications accordingly. As had become her habit, she asked me to read to her from her Bible.

"The Lord is my shepherd, I shall not be in want... Even though I walk through the valley of the shadow of death, I will fear no evil, for you are with me,"[5] I read from Psalm 23.

---

[5] Psalm 23 Verses 1 & 4

"I know the Lord is with me," she stated. "He never leaves me. He's given me a wonderful family. I'm so grateful to Him."

I admired her fortitude in my heart. She never complained. She counted every day a blessing and gave thanks. It was an honour to accompany her on her journey.

Grismelda was so pleased with the improvement in her ulcer that she came to the health centre once a week for us to inspect it and dress it, even though she lived an hour's drive away. She was still under the care of the hospital, but liked us to dress the tumour and help with other problems as they cropped up. She felt so much better that she believed the ulcer was decreasing in size. (As it was under her arm she could not see it.) The reality was that although we were controlling the smell and discomfort, the ulcer itself was slowly getting bigger. Little by little the ulcer was eroding the flesh under her arm and making an ever expanding hole.

Her arm also gave her a lot of trouble. It was so swollen that she could not move it. It hurt. It was prone to infection. Every time she came she appeared that bit thinner. However her spirit remained incredibly strong. Hortencia struck up a great relationship with her, encouraging her on the days she felt down. What we could do for her was very little in reality, but I think just the fact we gave her time, listened to her complaints and offered her some hope, gave her the lift she needed to carry on fighting another day. She knew she was not alone. She was determined to fight right to the very end.

I used to see her come week after week, and think what a privilege it was to be the person she had chosen to put her trust in during this most difficult time of her life. She did not demand the impossible from us. She did not waste energy berating her fate. She humbly accepted what life had handed out to her and tried her best to make every moment count.

One Saturday, Señora Muñoz's daughter telephoned and asked if I could go and see her that day, as she had taken a turn for the worse. Vladimir was home and the car was available, so I went along. I found Señora Muñoz now dozing in bed, only able to speak with a lot of effort and in a whisper. I took her hand and told her who I was. She immediately squeezed my hand and nodded her head slightly. I asked if she was in pain, and she shook her head, indicating that she felt comfortable, just very, very weary. Making a great effort she asked me to read to her from her Bible, and to sing her a hymn.

I found John 14 and read the words of Jesus, tears choking my voice, "In my Father's house there are many rooms I am going there to prepare a place for you."[6] Then her daughter, granddaughter and I quietly sang a hymn to her and prayed for her. It was a beautiful moment. Señora Muñoz was at peace and ready to leave this world. We were all in tears, but mostly thankful to have had the chance to know this affectionate grandmother and mother.

The next day her daughter phoned me to tell me that Señora Muñoz had died that night. My memories of her and her family were full of warmth, love and unity. She was a true example of humility before the

---

[6] John 14 Verse 2

Lord and of great courage. Accompanying her in her last months of life was indeed a great privilege and a blessing to me and to Hortencia.

Even as I realised that God does not always protect us from suffering, so I discovered that He gives us the wonderful gift of His presence, at all times, even in the most difficult circumstances. God became Immanuel to me: "God with us". As God gave me His comfort, His strength and His hope so I, simply by accompanying the sick, could also offer them this same solace. I discovered there was great value in simply being with another human-being in their time of need. I was learning that God is present with us through the lives of others.

CHAPTER 8

THE ALL-SUFFICIENT-ONE

"You know, living in a place where I am constantly aware of the dangers and suffering around me, means that I'm also reminded daily of my need to rely on God. I rely on myself when everything's easy, predicable and under control. I feel no need of God," I commented to Vladimir one morning.

"Well, that's one way of looking at it I suppose," he said, perhaps not feeling the same vulnerability, as he had grown up with the insecurities and calamities. They were part of his normality.

"No really," I emphasized, "I feel very privileged to be more aware of my vulnerability and weakness. I think I can finally understand Jesus' words in the beatitudes.[7] He said that it was the poor, the hungry, the sorrowful and the hated that were blessed in the kingdom of Heaven. I think those who have least, those who suffer and sorrow, naturally fix their sights on their Saviour and His promises of a brighter, eternal future."

---

[7] Matthew 5 Verses 3-12

"Jesus also said that those who are least in this life will be first in the next. I think suffering makes us look forward to eternity, and focus on that which has eternal value," Vladimir commented.

"That's it exactly. The poor are not so bogged down in the complications of life here and now as I am. The more I have, the more I have to worry about, and the more I rely on myself. I have so many things to think about here on earth, I don't have time to reflect on the eternal. Yet it's the hope of eternity that sustains me when loved ones depart: the hope of being reunited with them again one day."

This experience of being out of my comfort zone, mingling with the poor and needy, struggling with the spectre of suffering, led to a new understanding of God. In times of need, He truly was Immanuel. When I was perplexed and troubled, He was my Wonderful Counsellor. When I felt weak and impotent, He was Mighty God. When I was afraid and alone, He was my Everlasting Father. When I was eaten up by inner conflicts, He was the Prince of Peace.[8]

I stopped relying on myself so much. I needed help from others to cope from day to day. This, in turn, made me more aware of my need to depend on God. Being a missionary was somewhat different to being a doctor in the NHS, where my bank account had been amply replenished every month. People most generously donated to Project Ecuador to sponsor their child, to provide medicines or spectacles for the needy, or to build houses for the poor. There were also other friends

[8] Isaiah 9 Verse 6

who donated money that was specifically for our support. These people enabled us to continue working for the charity instead of having to look for other paid work.

"I got another email from a friend who can't support us anymore," I commented to Vladimir. "She's having a baby and isn't working now. To tell the truth, I can barely make ends meet at the moment. We could do with another donor or two."

"The problem is the plants on the farm are still very young. There are no large flowers to take to the florists to sell yet. I'm still buying them from the lady up the road to keep the customers," Vladimir reminded me. "It should get better in a few months."

"I hope so. It just makes me wonder how sustainable living here is. The price of everything keeps going up. Tamara's about to start going to nursery, which will cost money. Educating the girls is going to be a challenge here. Maybe we'll have to think about going to Britain and getting jobs at some point. Our income seems to go down, while the cost of living goes up!"

"Let's wait and see how things go with the farm. I hope we can make a go of it. It just takes time. Otherwise, I'll have to get a job somewhere else," Vladimir reflected. "God will help us find a way."

When patients like Grismelda came to the health centre, I was ashamed of my worrying. She relied on God in the midst of much greater problems than I had. Each time she came, she was weaker and the ulcer was bigger. Although it appeared impossible, her right arm seemed more swollen. Then her face and left arm became swollen. The hospital had already said there was nothing more they could do for the swelling, so I gave her the medicines I could, with some improvement. Nevertheless, it was very distressing to see her suffering. Hortencia continued to do a wonderful job of caring for her.

"How are you today, dear Grismelda?" she asked, and then listened to her reply with great attention.

"My arms feel so heavy. But I can breathe much easier again now the swelling has gone down a bit with the medicine the doctor gave me. I need some more of those tablets, I think. I have this patch on, from the hospital, for the pain. It's difficult to get comfortable in bed. My cousin does a great job helping me."

"The doctor will give you more medicine, don't worry. How's the ulcer today?"

"That's not bothering me much at all. You do a great job dressing it. You have magic hands."

"And how are your family, your husband and your sons?" Hortencia enquired.

"They're well thank you. My sons are doing well in their jobs and one has just announced he's going to get married soon. I'm very pleased. She's a lovely girl. She will be good for him."

After I spoke to Grismelda and saw how she relied on God while her life was slipping away, I reproached myself for not believing God would provide for my needs also.

The next day brought Señora Maria to our gate. I was busy feeding Emily and Tamara, so Vladimir went to see what she wanted. I had known Señora Maria ever since I had first arrived in Santo Domingo. She was the mother of eight children. The eldest, Esther, had married aged fourteen and now had two children of her own. The oldest two boys had left primary school, aged eighteen, without finishing. The rest had sponsors so that they could attend school. Señora Maria's husband had abandoned her for a year when I was first in the village, and to everyone's disappointment had then returned, promptly causing her problems in her health and home.

The community had helped Señora Maria in many ways. They had given her a plot of land, a free connection to the water system of the village and many heads of bananas. Her husband spent most of his time down at the village shop, drinking and smoking any money he made.

One evening, the neighbours had had to intervene when he had tried to strangle her. With support, she had reported him to the domestic violence office and had obtained a document forbidding him to return to the house. However, within weeks she had allowed him back.

Vladimir, with donations given to Project Ecuador, had built them a house. They had been living in a wooden shack with more gaps in the walls than you could count. Water ran through the house in the rainy season. The floor was mud. The roof was part rusty zinc and part plastic. The children had been suffering. The new house was made of blocks. It had a cement floor and new zinc roof, a toilet and a shower. They were protected from the elements much better. I wondered what Señora Maria needed that day.

"Señora Maria says she needs help for the children at school," Vladimir came to the door with the tiny, dark woman. She gave me a big hug and a kiss, and wished me God's blessing.

"Please can you help me with money to pay for the food the school gives the children at break time?" she asked. "I often have to send them to school without eating any breakfast, so I want them to have food at school, but I can't afford to pay for it."

"How much is it?" I enquired.

"It's five dollars per child this term," she informed me.

"Yes, I can help you with that from the sponsorship money," I assured her. "Just make sure you ask for a receipt at the school when you pay. You must bring me the receipt."

I was concerned about the children. They lived such chaotic lives and did not have food to eat every meal time. Señora Maria was part of the sewing group, which gave her some income to help buy food. She went to a church that insisted she gave a donation every week and that required the children to fast. She took the children to meetings late at night during the week, so they fell asleep at school the next day. She said she received prophesies and visions. Before I had gone to Scotland for Emily's birth, she had solemnly warned me that there was going to be an earthquake in Britain and that I should not go. Some mornings, when I was attending patients in the health centre, I could hear her shouting hymns at the top of her voice in frenzy.

At Christmas, I had given her a radio, as she had once said how much she longed to be able to hear the hymns play on the radio. Later I regretted it, when I heard that her husband had been beating the children with the flex from the radio.

Jacqueline was now sixteen years old and in her first year of secondary school. She was the first in her family to have finished primary school, so I was very proud of her achievement. She was a simple girl, somewhat immature for her age, but very good natured. She had to help her mother look after the four younger children. I wondered what future she had in store.

The desperate needs of families such as Señora Maria's made my worries pale in comparison, and yet the pressures of life were not to be ignored. Vladimir and I went out the next morning in the hunt for a suitable nursery for Tamara. Nursery was a relatively new concept in Santo Domingo. Most three-year-olds stayed at home with their mother, as few worked outside the home. Otherwise, Granny would help out when needed. The government had just announced its plans to make school compulsory from the age of four. Preschool education was becoming a priority. Nurseries and kindergartens were attached to primary schools and children usually progressed up on through the same school, so we wanted to find one that would hopefully suit Tamara for several years to come.

The fact that no other British parent I knew had educated their child in a school in Santo Domingo, niggled at the back of my mind. All of them had considered the education inadequate in some way and had either moved to Quito or to Britain. I wanted to find out more for myself.

The local state schools did not have nurseries, so they were ruled out automatically. I also knew the classes in these schools were forty to fifty pupils per teacher. I could see Tamara being lost amongst so many other children. The new flag-ship government "Millennium" school had an impossibly long waiting list. So we went to investigate the private schools. There were many such institutions in Santo Domingo and most of them were not too expensive. The first we tried was the nearest. It declared itself to be a Montessori school. We looked around with interest.

"What time do the children have to be here by?" I asked the young woman who was showing us round.

"They come at nine in the morning and go home at two in the afternoon. This is the classroom for the three-year-olds." She showed us a small room with books laid out on the floor and toys on the shelves. "They do gardening some days and go swimming in the pool. We have a music classroom over here and computers that the older children use over there."

"How many children do you have in a class?" I asked.

"No more than twenty. Some of the classes are smaller," the woman replied.

"And how much are the monthly fees?" Vladimir pitched in.

"They're around three hundred dollars a month, depending on the age of the child."

Once we were outside Vladimir and I raised our eye-brows. "Well, that's a bit more than we can afford!" I exclaimed.

"Anyway, Tamara digs up the garden at home and we take her swimming in the river. We don't need a school that does all that," Vladimir pointed out.

"Very true. Let's try the next one," I agreed.

We went on to consider a couple of Christian schools on the outskirts of the city, but they too were pricey and they would have meant leaving the house at six-thirty in the morning to get Tamara there for the half-seven start time.

"I'm not getting up at five o'clock in the morning with a little baby to look after as well," I said, point blank refusing.

"My mother got up at that time all her life, to cook the rice and give us breakfast before we left for school," Vladimir remonstrated.

"Well, not when you were three years old," I replied. "Tamara, Emily and I need our rest!"

"Where else is there we can look at?" Vladimir asked.

"There's the one our side of town. Sayuri goes there and gets on well. Let's go and look at it."

When we arrived the Head-teacher took us into her office to chat.

"The three-year-olds come from eight in the morning until noon," she explained to us. "We have no more than twenty children in the class. The fees are fifty dollars a month. There's also the registration fee, and uniform and books to buy."

"I think this is the nursery to go for. At least it's within our budget. The head was very friendly and the class size is small," I commented to Vladimir as we left.

"They don't have much space. I think the classrooms are a bit cramped. But, yes, I think it's the most practical," Vladimir agreed.

"I'm a bit nervous about sending her," I confessed, "but I think she'll enjoy being with the other children and doing the art and games."

"She's so little still," Vladimir began to get sentimental. "But I do think she'll enjoy it."

The start of term was just a few weeks away, so I began to get together the things Tamara was going to need. I paid the registration fee, bought shoes and plimsolls and uniform, but still had the first month's fees to pay and the list of stationary items to buy. It included everything from crayons, paper, paint and art materials to toilet rolls, a toothbrush and a cushion. If I was struggling to be able to afford all this in one go, I could totally understand why poor children needed a sponsor in order to be able to afford all these items.

"I hope we're doing the right thing," I shared with Vladimir. "I want the girls to have an education that will enable them to live in Britain in the future if they want to. I suppose I could teach them at home, but for me there's no point being in Santo Domingo if I can't do the charity work. I don't see how I could teach the girls and keep working as a doctor as well. I'm prepared to live here with the current level of risk and threats, as I don't think the girls are in physical danger. But, when push comes to shove, I won't sacrifice their education."

"Children should go to school," Vladimir retorted. "Tamara will be fine. I had all my education in Santo Domingo. Stop worrying so much!"

I swallowed my doubts and put on a brave face for Tamara's sake. I did want her to enjoy being with the other children. I continued to pray we would have enough to pay the fees and gave thanks each week when we had enough to pay our shopping bill. Having been brought up in a fiercely independent society, I was reluctant to tell others we were struggling. Learning to rely on God, who knew our every need, was one thing, but receiving help from the people around me was a harder lesson to learn.

CHAPTER 9

LIVING IN COMMUNITY

I felt I was in the middle of a gale of emotions, being blown this way and that by the desires of my heart. One moment, I was in the peaceful place of contentment with what I had. The next, conflict filled my mind, buffeting me from all sides. Just as I had reconciled myself to living with the dangers we were exposed to, I faced a new challenge. Like any parent, I wanted the best for my girls. Could I give them that in Santo Domingo? Wouldn't they be better off in Britain, with me earning a good salary, able to send them to an excellent school, such as the one I myself had attended? Ashamed, I wondered why I was worrying about them having the best of everything, when the other children in the village could not even afford to attend their local school. And yet, didn't having a British mother have to mean something as well? Vladimir was very laid back about education, but he did not have anything to compare it to. I was yet to be convinced.

My mind in a whirl, I popped Emily into her baby carrier and grabbed Tamara's hand as we went out of the gate to wait for the bus. Vladimir needed the car on the farm most days, so we were catching the bus to nursery. As the bus came, we quickly jumped on and clung on. I gripped Tamara with one hand and the rail above my head with the other. The fifteen-minute ride passed quickly as we swayed our way to the school. Tamara was settling in very well. She was happy to stay, had made little friends and joined in everything. The drop-off was easy. Then I had to wait for half an hour for the bus back to the health centre. It meant I was late for work.

The return journey to pick her up was worse, as the bus times did not coincide at all. It was proving a little tricky. Sometimes, Vladimir could come and pick her up. Sometimes, a friend could lend me their car. This was a life saver. Other times, I just had to leave work early to be at the school gates on time. A car of my own was becoming a necessity.

The price of rice had gone up yet again. Milk, yoghurt, meat, and chicken crept up in price month by month. All imported goods had a new, heavy tax on them and were outside our budget. The weekly shop was becoming a stressful exercise.

To my surprise, the first way God helped us through this difficult time was through my patients. I had gone to Ecuador to help the poor. Now I found I needed to learn to receive from them too. Felicita was a diabetic patient who had been faithfully attending the health centre for years. Month by month, we gave her the medications she needed for free through the donations of a Bible study group in Britain. One Friday, she brought me a chicken as a thank-you gift. I was truly grateful as I did not have any meat left for us to eat that week. The next week, another diabetic patient who we helped with free medicines, brought me some apples and pomegranates, as she knew they were favourites of the girls. A few days later, the friends of Grismelda, who were fish wholesalers, brought me a bagful of fresh fish. These gifts kept us going. God knew our needs and was able to meet them in His time and way, even as we tried to help those who were so much worse off than ourselves. I was so used to being the one who bestowed gifts upon others that it was humbling to be on the receiving end for a change. It was typical of life in Ecuadorian society where people still lived in community, helping each other out whenever they saw the need. It was a lesson I needed to learn.

* * *

Señora Maria came to the sewing group full of woe. "Dear doctor, dear doctor, I need to speak to you," she exclaimed, taking me to one side. At first, I could not understand her garbled account, but as she calmed down a little and started to tell me a slower version of events, I began to get the gist of what she was trying to tell me.

"It's my eldest daughter Esther," she began. "She was home last evening alone with her two little girls, when a man came to the door. She let him in and he had a bag over his head, so she could not see his face. He beat her and then ran off. She knew it was her husband though. She recognised his voice. He's beaten her often before, but now she doesn't want to put up with it anymore. She's afraid of him. She came to my house with the girls. Can you give her some sewing so that she can earn some money?" Esther had accompanied her Mum with her two preschool girls. She looked at me expectantly.

"Have you reported this to the authorities?" I asked looking at the bruises Esther was trying to hide under her hair and hat.

"No, not yet," Señora Maria shook her head sadly. "We don't have the money to pay for the bus to get to town."

"Will you go, if I ask Fred next door to take you in his car?" I questioned.

They both nodded. "Yes, we don't want this to go on any longer."

"Let's do that first then," I responded. I paid Señora Maria for her sewing, so that she had something to buy the family food with. She now had seven sons and daughters and two grandchildren under her roof in a three-bedroom house, not to mention her husband, who would no doubt return home worse for wear later that evening. I also gave them a bag of eggs a patient had given me that day and some cooking bananas from the farm. Fred very kindly gave them a lift to the domestic violence office and Esther reported her husband. I wondered what was going to happen next.

Grismelda came to the health centre the next day. I apologised for arriving late, after dropping Tamara off at nursery. The bus had not come, so I had ended up having to get a taxi.

"Doctor, the swelling in my neck and face isn't bothering me too much," she began. "At least they are not affecting my breathing at the moment. My arms do feel so heavy and ungainly. I can hardly move the right one at all. But I have a new problem. I spend so much time lying on my back, that the skin is sore there."

I looked at her with great compassion. Despite her brave façade, her face was very swollen and must have been uncomfortable. Her arms were almost grotesque. They were so swollen, water droplets formed on the outside of her skin. It was because her arms were so unwieldy that she could not move position much, or be moved by her attentive family. Very few positions were comfortable. As I looked at the base of her spine, I saw a pressure sore was forming.

Hortencia bathed and dressed the wound. "You've lost more weight," Hortencia commented gently.

"I can't eat much at the moment," Grismelda explained. "The strong medicines they give me at the hospital for the pain make me feel sick."

I could imagine that the swelling did not enable her to swallow much either. The advanced disease in itself was making her waste away day by day.

Grismelda's friend took me aside. "She's been staying with us this week, as she finds the hour-long journey to her own home too difficult now. She wants to go home today. Should we take her? She looks too weak to travel."

"You must know that she doesn't have much time left in this world. Let her do what she wants to. Let her be with the people she wants to be with. It's the best you can do for her now," I counselled.

"You know, if I were suffering as she is, I would want it to end," Grismelda's friend declared. "Grismelda still wants to live. I suppose she's so young. She's still hoping for improvement."

"She's incredibly brave," I replied. "She's still fighting this horrible disease. Listen to her and help her in whatever ways you can. She really appreciates your help and support. Enjoy her company and her friendship while you can."

As Grismelda was wheeled out in the wheelchair to the car, I wondered if I would ever see her again.

Esther was next into the consulting room. She had come to ask for financial help again. She wanted to join the sewing group. I was hesitant, because we were already struggling to sell all the goods we made. As I looked at her, I thought of her marrying aged fourteen to escape from unwanted attention at home. I remembered she was unable to read and write. I considered her two little girls and how her mother was in no position to help, and so agreed to let her sew while she looked for other work.

"Thank you so much doctor," Esther exclaimed, a smile coming to her lips at last. "This is really going to help me feed my girls. My oldest, Andrea, is due to start school in April. Do you think you would be able to find her a sponsor?"

"I can certainly try," I replied. "Which school will she be going to?"

Esther looked excited, as she thought about her daughter's future. "She'll go to the local school here in the village. I can't wait for her to start learning to read and write. I never had the chance."

That evening, I received some good news. A British friend of mine was going to England for a couple of months, and was willing to lend me her pick-up truck while she was away.

"This is going to make my life *so* much easier," I rejoiced to Vladimir. "I'll be able to get to work on time and pick up Tamara on time. I can do visits when

I need to and not have to wait until you don't need the car. This is going to be a great two months!"

"It will make your life much easier," Vladimir agreed. "Wouldn't it be great if we could get a little car for you."

"We need every cent we have at the moment. Maybe it will be possible one day," I replied, not believing it for a second. "I'm so glad I asked if I could borrow the pick-up truck. I wouldn't normally have dared. I'm scared I might damage it! Sometimes, necessity makes us take the plunge."

"I'm sure she's happy to lend it to you," Vladimir reassured me. "It's good to help each other out and to share."

"I suppose I'm used to being the one who gives, not the one who receives," I admitted. "You Ecuadorians are much better at living in community and sharing what you have, than I am. Anyway, I'm going to make the most of it and be thankful. I'm also going to keep praying we have a little more income. It would really help."

CHAPTER 10

STAYING IN THE BATTLE

I began to realise that a large part of God's response to our suffering is found in community: in the kindness of those He has placed around us. As a doctor, my gut reaction was to want to fix all ills. Often this was simply not possible. Nevertheless, I found there was great meaning in being able to listen and speak, give and receive, weep and laugh with my patients and neighbours. I found meaning in simply staying in the battle, refusing to ignore the injustices I saw around me and continuing to participate in community life.

Señora Maria came running into the health centre in a panic one morning, to tell me her latest drama.

"Esther's husband arrived, while we were at the river washing clothes, and took their two little girls from the house. He's run off with another woman from the village and taken them to the jungle."

"Have you reported it?" I asked, my pulse racing, my palms sweating.

"Yes, but the police say there's nothing they can do, because the girls are with their father. Esther would have to go and find them herself in the jungle. She's never been there and doesn't know what to do." Señora Maria was at a loss. She wrung her hands and paced up and down the room, tears rolling down her cheeks.

"How can he just take them like that and not let them see their mother?" I asked aloud, not really expecting an answer. "What must those little girls be feeling? They've never spent a day away from their mother. How long is he intending to keep them from her?"

"Esther is just crying and crying in our house. She refuses to go out or do anything," Señora Maria worried, her distress mounting. "I don't know how to help her."

I did not know how to help them either, other than by praying. The whole situation seemed to be going from bad to a nightmare.

* * *

My other patients were, plain and simple, an inspiration. With the loan of the pick-up truck I was able to visit Señora Piedad regularly. She had been diagnosed with a tumour of her hard palate several years before, but had opted not to have it operated on because she was so scared by the surgeon's descriptions of tracheostomies and feeding tubes. She now lived with a grotesque, disfiguring tumour obliterating her face.

On our first visit, I could hardly believe my eyes. In all my years as a doctor, I had never seen anything like it. Her whole face was swollen, a large, bleeding, smelly mass, pushing out her nose and right eye, making anyone who looked at her likely to stare in revulsion.

One-year-old Emily was with me on the visit, but she was still young enough not to be bothered by Piedad's looks. She just gazed up at Piedad curiously and smiled sweetly at her. I took her hand to wish her a good-morning and then we sat down to chat. Piedad began the conversation.

"Señora Muñoz's daughter recommended you to us, Doctor," she began. "She told us you could help me like you helped her mother. Can you help me with this tumour?"

"Tell me more about it," I asked.

"I've had it for five years. They wanted to cut it away, but they said I would have to eat and breathe through tubes, so my family decided not to let me have the operation. I can't imagine living like that. And now I have lived so many more years! The tumour keeps growing though. It was not this big in the beginning. Now the constant watery-blood that runs from it bothers me. It itches like there are worms wriggling inside it. Sometimes it hurts, but not too much. Can you help me?"

"Yes I can help," I reassured her. "I can give you medicines to take away the itch and the pain, but I can't make it any smaller."

Hortencia dressed the tumour to control the bleeding and the smell, while we asked about Piedad's family.

"I have eight children and more grandchildren," Piedad told us with pride. "I like to go and visit them. They live in different places, so I travel around quite a bit. Next week I am going to Ambato to visit my son. Sometimes, I go to Guayaquil to visit my daughter."

"They are several hours journey away," I observed. "Do you go on the bus?"

"Yes," she affirmed. "I can still travel fine. It's just my face that bothers me."

I was impressed by her attitude. She did not mind strangers staring at her, as they surely must have done. She lived her life regardless.

"When can you come and see me again?" Piedad asked.

"How about we come when you are back from Ambato?" I suggested. "Then we can see how you are getting on with the new medications."

"That would be perfect," Piedad agreed.

I could see no reason why such a brave woman should be cursed with such a terrible illness. I could see no reason why I had been born into plenty, while others were born into want. Reflecting on these mysteries created in me a huge sense of thankfulness for the many blessings I enjoyed each and every day.

However, we could not live on thin air. I had cut down all our expenses to what I considered the bare minimum and was still struggling to pay the monthly bills. I was considering our situation, and was thinking of writing an appeal to those who received our prayer letters, asking directly for more support. We really needed a few new donors to replace those who had dropped out.

I was amazed when, without me saying a word to anyone, and before I formulated any letter of appeal, not one, but several generous people started supporting us.

"We have had five people start standing orders this month," my sister, the treasurer of Project Ecuador, informed me one afternoon on Skype. "They all want their money to go to your personal support. Isn't that great?"

Great? I was gobsmacked, incredulous. This had never happened to me before. It was always people having to stop supporting, not new people starting. The timing was perfect. It was God's gift to us. It was a confirmation I was in the right place, doing the right thing. It was as if I felt my Heavenly Father's loving arms around me urging me to stay in the battle, to keep helping those who were suffering.

"That's amazing," I replied in awe. "I was beginning to think we would have to come home or find other work. How incredible that they have come forward of their own accord, without me asking for new support. I think I'm going to cry!"

"Hey, God will provide all you need," my sister assured me. "He loves you very much."

I got on my knees to thank Him for His provision, and for doing it in this way. I choked up, as I realised that the money had been offered without me having to ask, just when I needed it. It was an expression of God's unconditional, overflowing love. It was a loving Father giving good gifts to His children. I felt humbled by His grace and greatly loved by Him and precious to Him.

In Scotland, my mother had been busy raising funds for a car for me. Her Girls' Brigade did a sponsored walk, she sold bric-a-brac, and others too rallied to the cause. The day she sent me a text message to say a family friend had donated one thousand pounds towards a car was another breath-taking moment. People were so kind and generous. God was good. I was so very, very thankful for this provision. I felt part of the wider community of God's people. Christians the other side of the world were helping their fellow-man in Ecuador through their generosity. In doing so, they too were staying in the battle against evil and suffering.

Vladimir and I went to the second-hand car market in Quito to hunt for a suitable vehicle. We wandered through the rows and rows of cars asking the year they were made and the asking price. There were hundreds of vehicles: big and small, new and old. The hot sun beat down on us relentlessly, as we walked in the heat of the day. I became quite dizzy looking at all the vehicles on offer. Eventually, we found a Ford Fiesta owned by a couple from Otavalo. They were indigenous people who made wonderful handicrafts and exported their products all over the world. This couple were in need of a larger vehicle, so wanted to sell the small car.

Vladimir went to the local Police Station to check the car had not been stolen, and then asked a mechanic to look it over to check its general condition. The next day, the couple brought it to Santo Domingo, where we signed the contract at a solicitor's office. It was fascinating chatting to the couple who spoke the Quichua language, as well as Spanish, and who had travelled to the USA and Europe selling their wares. The man was dressed in his typical poncho and hat, with a long plait down his back. His wife was dressed in a thick, woollen, wrap-around skirt and a beautifully embroidered blouse. I wondered how they bore the heat of Santo Domingo while dressed so warmly. Their home-town Otavalo, high in the Andes Mountains, had a much colder climate. Their culture was very different to their compatriots in Santo Domingo. It struck me anew what a varied country Ecuador is.

I drove home in our new car ecstatic to have wheels of my own. I thanked God every day for the blessing of that car. I made snazzy car-seat-covers from denim, adorned with bright flowers, to protect the seats from the dust and dirt of Santo Domingo, and installed the girls' car-seats with pride. We now had a girl-mobile.

* * *

Esther came to see me in the health centre. She looked so young. She was not yet out of her teenage years, and she had already gone through so much. The family had lived in the back-of-beyond looking after a farm when she was a child, which was why she had not had the chance to go to school. She had leapt from the frying pan into the fire, when she had abandoned her abusive step-father, aged fourteen, to marry a violent man. Now, she had lost her two daughters and was in distress.

"Could you not go to the jungle to try and find your girls?" I asked. Even as I said the words, I wondered where she would find the money to do so, and if she had ever travelled outside of Santo Domingo before. Esther looked embarrassed and kept her gaze downcast.

"That's why I've come. I'm pregnant. My husband isn't the father," Esther confessed.

"How far along are you?" I asked, concerned for her and the baby.

"About three months I think," she replied, looking up at me for the first time.

"And what does the father say?" I enquired.

"I haven't told him yet," Esther shook her head, perplexed by her situation. "I've been left with nothing, and I've no means of caring for a baby by myself. I can't find work. I don't even know how to read and write. What will become of us?" She started to weep.

"It's my nephew, isn't it?" Hortencia intervened. Esther nodded and looked at Hortencia in a quizzical manner through her tears.

"Let me come with you to talk to him. I'm sure he will want to take care of you and the baby."

"Would you do that for me?" Esther asked in wonder. She was not used to people being willing to help her.

"Of course I will." Hortencia assured her in a motherly fashion. "We will go and find him when he finishes work this afternoon. He's working for my husband, weeding the pineapple field today."

I examined Esther, gave her request forms so that she could have an ultrasound and blood tests done, and sent her away with some vitamins. Hortencia, the soul of kindness, kept her promise in the afternoon.

Leaving the health centre at midday, I drove calmly to pick up Tamara from nursery, feeling so thankful I now had a car. Things seemed to be going well. I waited with the other mums at the gate until the little three-year-olds spilled out of their classroom and came running towards us, eager to see their mummies. Tamara clamoured at the gate, while the teacher unlocked it.

"Mummy, they pricked me today with a needle," she cried, showing me her arm.

"What do you mean?" I asked.

"The nurses came from the health department and vaccinated all the children today," the teacher informed us. "I think it was for the 'flu." As we retrieved our children, she handed us each a small slip of paper, which stated they had in fact been vaccinated against yellow fever. Apparently, there was a campaign on against the virus, after an outbreak amongst the soldiers in the jungles. The Department of Health saw no need to consult the parents of the children as to whether their children could be vaccinated. They just did it.

"But Vladimir, they shouldn't just arrive and vaccinate children without their parents' consent!" I protested later. "They don't know if the child has already had the vaccine. They don't know if they have any allergies, and I know they don't carry any epinephrine to treat an allergic reaction were one to occur. They don't know if the child has had another vaccine in the previous month. Some parents might not want their child vaccinated, because of the risk of side-effects. They should ask for consent."

"It doesn't work like that here," Vladimir replied shrugging his shoulders. "I've never heard of anyone having a reaction. People here die of infectious diseases and are grateful that the government gives them vaccines for free. No one is going to complain about it."

"People do also have reactions sometimes," I retorted. "A few years back, a couple came to my gate late at night, with their baby fitting in their arms after he had been vaccinated. I was in a meeting at the hospital once, where they were organising an influenza vaccination campaign, going house to house vaccinating the elderly. When someone asked what to do about an allergic reaction the instructor just said to find a neighbour with a car and send them to the hospital as fast as they could. That could well be too late. I do think vaccination is important, but the needs of individuals are too."

"The government is more concerned about preventing these life-threatening illnesses in the millions, than worrying about one or two who might have a bad reaction. Here, the government has the right to insist on vaccination. To be registered in a school in the first place, you have to show your vaccination card to prove your child has had all their immunizations. It's compulsory. No Ecuadorian is going to complain about that. We see it as the government taking care of us."

"I just can't believe it!" I was not convinced. "I should decide what does and doesn't happen to my own daughter. Is it likely to happen again?"

"Yes, of course," Vladimir replied. "Schools are the ideal place to find the majority of children. Whenever there's a campaign, the nurses will turn up and vaccinate them. The school doesn't know they are coming. They just arrive, line up the children and stick the needles in."

"Just as I thought all was going well, this has to happen!" I thought to myself. I began to wonder if having Tamara in an Ecuadorian school was such a good idea after all. Were there other things the government was going to do to her, or teach her, without my knowledge or consent? Would I ever be able to relax, assured that all was well? Did I just have to accept Ecuadorians did things differently? What price was I willing to pay to stay in the battle in Ecuador?

CHAPTER 11

IN SEARCH OF SERENITY

Every day, I was exposed to different ways of doing things, as my patients and neighbours told me of the events in their lives. I had long ago come to accept that British customs were not necessarily any worse or any better. We just had different perspectives on life. As I was the stranger amongst the Ecuadorians, I tried to fit in as best I could. I searched for "serenity to accept the things I could not change, courage to change the things I could, and wisdom to know the difference."[9] As I did so, I discovered new insights into my patients' faith in God in the midst of their suffering.

Grismelda's friends came to the health centre. Grismelda was not with them. We were never to see her brave, smiling face again.

"Grismelda died last week," they informed us. "The swelling of her face got worse again and she went into a coma and died two days later. We were at the wake. All her family were so sad, but also relieved. She was so ill by the end. It was hard to see her in so much pain and discomfort. The wake was good. We all got to see

---

[9] The Serenity Prayer attributed to Reinhold Niebuhr

her resting in her coffin. Even the children looked in the coffin to say good-bye. Grismelda always appreciated coming here. She wanted us to bring her right up to her last days. You always gave her time and hope."

"We're sorry to hear of her passing," Hortencia and I agreed. "She was such a strong lady. We will always remember her. It's sad she won't live to see her sons married or to care for her grandchildren."

"It's God's will. We have to look to the future," Grismelda's friend remarked. "Her son has a wedding to look forward to. Soon there will be a baby, and life will go on. We have to keep going forwards, not dwell on the past. Of course, she will always be missed. She was a dear friend."

Esther came in next with Hortencia's nephew, who was nicknamed 'the devil' by his mates in the village. I hoped he did not live up to his name.

"We've come so you can give me a check-up and see the results of the ultrasound scan," Esther informed me. "Steven wants to make sure I'm OK."

I ushered them in and gave them a seat, while I looked at the scan. Everything seemed to be going just fine. "You are doing fine and so is the baby," I assured them. "Are you still living with your Mum?"

"Steven and I have made a little room at the back of her house, and we're living there at the moment. It's not much, but at least we're out of the rain there."

I had seen the makeshift wooden shack, and knew it was barely a dwelling at all. I hoped they were sufficiently protected. I was glad Steven was being responsible and providing for Esther and the baby. At least she had food to eat, and someone to pay for the ultrasound and other tests she would need.

"I hope my girls are being well cared for in the jungle." Esther sighed. "I miss them so much, but I have to think of this new little one on the way now."

I left the health centre early that morning, in order to pay Piedad a visit. We went to a different house this time, as she was now staying with her eldest daughter. The yard had puppies, chickens and ducks roaming around it, all making a noise. Inside the house was a very old sofa, with lumpy cushions. A damp smell hung in the air. We sat down gingerly and waited for Piedad to come out of her room, where she was taking a nap. Her grandson, who looked like he was about eight years old, sat on the sofa too, watching a cartoon on their tiny television. As I looked around the room, I saw a glass cage filled with larvae and tiny black beetles.

"What are those beetles for?" I asked the cute, chubby boy curiously.

"Oh they're my Mum's," the boy replied casually. "She eats them."

"Why does she eat them?" I asked, raising my eyebrows.

"They're good for gastritis and all kinds of illnesses, like stopping you getting cancer." The boy was very matter of fact. "You start by eating one a day and then eat more each day until you are eating seventy a day."

"Seventy?" I exclaimed. "What do they taste like?"

"Oh, I don't know." The boy shrugged as only eight-year-olds can. "Just my Mum eats them. She had gastritis and now she's better." He turned back to his cartoon, which was obviously much more interesting to him than beetles.

Just then, Piedad came shuffling out of her room and joined us on the sofa. Dabbing at her dripping tumour, she gave both Hortencia and I a warm hug.

"Thank you for coming to see me," she exclaimed. "How are you, doctor?"

"I'm well, thank you," I replied. "We've come to see how you are. How did you get on with your trip to Ambato?"

"I got on very well. The medicines did help me feel better. But now they've run out and my face feels like there are worms inside it again. It's the most awful feeling."

"Well, we can give you more medicines, if they helped," I said. "How long have you been back for?"

"Nearly two weeks I think. I was in the hospital because I had a haemorrhage and they had to give me some blood. My daughter donated me a pint of blood."

"And has it been bleeding again since then?" I asked.

"No, no Doctor, just weeping water coloured with blood, like it usually does."

Hortencia dressed Piedad's tumour while we talked, and we gave her some more medicines. Piedad really appreciated us taking the time to visit her and spend time with her. The more I got to know her, the more I marvelled at her acceptance of her condition. She never once complained or questioned God's purposes. She maintained her faith in a God of love. I repented of my pride in thinking I deserved a pain-free life. I came to God with a new humility, marvelling at His mercy towards me as He sustained me and protected me day by day.

Leaving Piedad, I went to collect Tamara from nursery. She was practising to be a Tsachila Indian, in a show which the nursery was putting on for the parents to celebrate the Santo Domingo annual festival. I was glad she had the opportunity to join in with other children and to learn about the local culture.

"You need to make her a Tsachila costume," Tamara's teacher informed me. "She'll be in the dance we're doing."

"What's the costume like?" I asked.

"You need the traditional, brightly-coloured, stripy skirt and a short, white top with something sparkly sewn on it. Then make her a head-band with different coloured ribbons streaming from it. We will paint black lines on them, as the Indians do, with face paints on the day."

I went to the market to get the right material, and sewed the skirt. I cut up an old sleeveless T-shirt, and sewed on some pink sequins. Once Tamara had them on, together with the colourful head-band, she looked quite the indigenous Indian.

On the day of the show, Vladimir and I, ever the proud parents, were there to watch. Emily bouncing on my knee, we sat near the front to get a good view. Tamara came out with her classmates, all enjoying themselves as Tsachila dancers. The boys were dressed in the traditional black and white striped skirts and painted, red hair. They all dipped and bobbed their way around the floor, some of them in time to the marimba music. We all applauded wildly. It was wonderful for us to see our first daughter growing and developing in so many ways.

I felt it was such a privilege to be able to live in this neglected corner of the world and have something to offer the sick and the needy. I wanted to stay in the battle. I hoped against hope the girls' need for a good education was not going to bring my vocation to an end.

* * *

Señora Maria's frenzied singing became louder every morning. We could not ignore it. The strident sound penetrated the walls, as we attended the patients in the health centre. The chanting grew more and more agitated as the days went by. Prayers were shouted to the heavens at the top of her voice. Her five youngest children were made to join in whenever they were not in school. I was concerned she was becoming unstable, so I went to visit her.

As I approached the little block house we had built the family a couple of years previously, I saw the tiny wooden shack tottering out the back, where Esther and Steven were expecting their baby. It was hardly fit to keep animals in, let alone human beings. I hoped they would be able to find something better soon.

Señora Maria greeted me with a fierce hug and kiss. "Dear Doctor, thank you for coming to see me. How are you?"

"I'm fine, thank you," I replied, "I was wondering how you are?"

"I'm worried about my children. They go without regular meals. I don't know how we're going to survive and what's going to happen to us. Last night, the wind blew just before the rains started and frightened us. Thank you for our house. The rain no longer comes in, but the roof banged in the wind and made so much noise I thought the world was coming to an end. I saw it in a vision. There's going to be an earthquake. We must pray so that the Lord does not destroy us all."

"Is there anything you need today?" I asked her gently.

"I've no food to cook the children for lunch when they come home," Señora Maria shook her head. "My husband's worse than useless. He does nothing for his children. It's thanks to you that they go to school. He doesn't care for them."

"Is he working at the moment?" I asked.

"No he didn't find work this week," she replied. "He's just down at the shop, smoking."

"Well, if he's agreeable, tell him to go and work on our farm the rest of the week. Come with me to the shop now and buy what you need for lunch. I will pay the bill from his wages on Saturday."

Señora Maria abandoned her frenzied praying and came with me. The children ate that day. Her husband started to work for us on the farm fairly regularly and to contribute to the upkeep of his children. Señora Maria calmed down a lot.

"I saw you in a dream," Señora Maria told me. "You were walking down the street looking pretty, and I was dressed in dirty rags. But you stopped and spoke to me and hugged me and gave me some food. I felt the love of Jesus."

I wept.

CHAPTER 12

WE NEED ONE ANOTHER

We need one another. God has given us each other to help one another in our times of trouble. These were some of the lessons I was learning, as I observed the people around me respond to the daily suffering in their lives.

Treating mental illness in Santo Domingo was difficult. There were medicines available, if not the latest and the best. The problem was the lack of infrastructure to care for people with serious mental illness. Those who are the sickest do not think they need to take medicines. The burden was on families and communities.

Justo had schizophrenia. He began to talk to himself, and to gesticulate at thin air, when he was a teenager. His parents died young, so it was down to his brother to care for him. He did so for several years, making sure that Justo took his medicine regularly, but with time it became more challenging. The brother married, and had children, and did not have the money to buy the medicine any more. His wife tried to help care for Justo, but Justo thought she was evil and used to call her all kinds of offensive names. As he stopped taking medicine regularly, his paranoia increased and he thought the medicine was poison. He soon refused all medicines point-blank. He left home and began to wander up and down the road incessantly.

Justo lived on a farm away into the green pastureland, where the farmers kept cows for milking. He walked incredible distances every day, sometimes going from the farm right to the edge of town, which was some twenty kilometres. All the way, he went talking and waving to his non-existent friends. He was skinny and wiry, very strong and physically fit. His hair grew in wild tufts about his head and he wore the same clothes every day.

The first time I met Justo, I was on our farm with the girls, having a swim in the river. It was a hot, humid afternoon and the refreshing water was soothing our fractious tempers. Tamara was swimming with her armbands and Emily was splashing as I held her under her tummy. I was relieved to be in the cool.

Justo appeared out of nowhere on the bank of the river. He talked and waved his arms about constantly. I did not know who he was, and kept my distance nervously. I did not know if he was a thief coming to see what we had on the farm. He certainly appeared strange. Vladimir had gone to take the farm workers home after their day's work. I felt on high alert and I wished he would come back soon.

Justo took no notice of us at all. He was lost in his own world. I kept the girls close to me, as we warily continued our swim, until Justo simply went on his way with a last shout to the heavens. When Vladimir arrived, I told him about the strange man.

"Oh that will've been Justo," Vladimir smiled. "He's sick. We know his family well. They've lived here for

GUINEA PIG FOR BRUNCH

years. I heard that the brother was having trouble caring for Justo and that he was wandering around again. Sometimes he goes to my parents' house for food. He's harmless."

"It's hard for families, when they have a mentally ill relative isn't it?" I remarked. "In Britain, you can detain people who are so ill by force and give them treatment."

"Can you really do that?" Vladimir was amazed. "I suppose the State pays for it. Here it all depends on whether you have a family that can pay for it."

"Some of the treatments I've seen for such patients have been somewhat hair-raising anyway," I exclaimed. "Do you remember Señora Cordova was very depressed last year? In desperation, the family put her into a psychiatric clinic, where the doctor decided to sedate her. He claimed that she would wake up miraculously better. Unfortunately, they over-sedated her. She stopped breathing and spent three days in intensive care. They charged the family one thousand dollars a day for intensive care - even though it was the doctor's mistake that put her there. I couldn't believe it. It must have taken them months to pay off that medical bill, and I don't think Señora Cordova was any better for the experience."

"Well, Justo is well known to us all here. No one bothers him. We just let him wander up and down the road. When he wants to, my parents let him sleep in their shed. The neighbours all look out for him and give him food. You don't need to worry about him."

"It would be good to find some way to give him medicine again," I suggested.

"He went to see you once. You probably don't remember. He says you tried to poison him with the medicines you gave him, and refuses to go and see you again. He knows who you are," Vladimir laughed.

"We need community psychiatric nurses and for the government to provide the medicines and services for free," I shook my head. "It's a very difficult situation."

Maybe Justo was being looked out for in the local way, by the local community, but others sometimes fell through the holes in the social network. Jessica was nine years old. She lived with her mother and father on a remote farm, and had little contact with the outside world. Frequent absences from school meant that she had fallen behind.

One afternoon, Vladimir arrived home late. I was beginning to wonder what had happened to him, when he burst in the door.

"Sorry I was late," he exclaimed, "there's been a tragedy. Young Jessica arrived home from school today to find her mother had been shot dead. Jessica is now with my Mum. People are saying it must be a revenge attack, because Jessica's father deals in drugs."

"That's awful!" I exclaimed. "The poor girl must be traumatised. Where's her father?"

"No one knows at the moment. He's my aunt-by-marriage's brother, so he will be in touch with my aunt soon I should imagine. The police are investigating, so they can't do the wake yet."

"Did you know Jessica's mum?" I asked.

"Not really," Vladimir confessed. "Her father is such bad news, everyone keeps out of his way. His wife kept herself to herself, and hardly ever came out of the house. We usually just see Jessica on the days she goes to school. My mum is taking care of her at the moment. The poor girl has hardly any clothes and eats like a sparrow. I expect she'll stay with Mum for a few days, until her father makes contact."

Contrary to everyone's initial assumptions, the police concluded that Jessica's mother committed suicide. The funeral was a very small affair. Jessica's mother had come from Colombia when she married Jessica's father, and had not made friends in the village. She had been so very isolated and depressed. Her life was far from easy and, tragically, had been too much for her to cope with.

Jessica stayed with Vladimir's parents for a few weeks. They took her to town to buy her decent clothes and fed her many platefuls of nutritious soup. She played with Tamara and Emily and liked to feed the chickens and the guinea pigs which were being reared in the back-yard. Her father spoke with her aunt, who took Jessica in on a more permanent basis. We found Jessica a sponsor so that she could attend school regularly. The whole family took her under their wing and gradually she began to lose her mousey shyness, and to find her smile again. Soon, she was to be seen playing chase with the cousins like the rest of the children, laughter bubbling from her lips, although a wistful sadness never left her eyes.

No one really knew what her father was up to. He turned up occasionally, but was usually drunk, and his sister did not let him stay long in that state. Everyone told him to get his life in order, but no one expected him to do so. He was such a hard-nosed criminal, known to steal, traffic drugs, smoke drugs and drink and drink and drink. No one had ever seen such a person change for the better.

* * *

I was working as usual in the health centre, when there was a commotion outside. A woman fell into the clinic, accompanied by many other women all talking at once. Hortencia went out to find out what was causing the commotion.

"That madman threw a rock at the bus. It hit the windscreen and the glass cut her face!" one of the women informed us. "Look at her! She's bleeding."

We took the injured woman through to the consulting room and cleaned up her face. She had a long cut on her nose, which needed stitching. As I stitched, we asked more about what had happened.

"It was that man who always walks up and down the road talking to himself," one of the observers informed us. "He was just throwing his arms about and then he threw a rock. It's fortunate no one else was hurt. I don't think he meant to hurt anyone. He's not well is he?"

"Will this leave me with a scar?" the patient asked me. She was a well turned-out young woman who obviously took great pride in her appearance.

"It will heal well, but you will have a mark there," I tried to be reassuring. "You must keep it clean and dry until the stitches come out, so that it doesn't get infected. You will have the minimum of scarring."

The patient was trembling with shock. "It all happened so fast!" she exclaimed. "I never imagined something like that would happen to me."

"You're fine. That's the main thing," her friend consoled her. "The poor man isn't well. He didn't do it on purpose."

"Oh, I know. I just hope he doesn't do it again," she replied with a short laugh, no bitterness or rancour in her voice.

The next patient to come in was a neighbour, bringing her baby who had a cold. She had seen the commotion and the wounded woman.

"Justo is harmless," she commented. "He would never do that on purpose. I don't think he will do it again. It was just unfortunate." This was the general consensus, and Justo continued to wander up and down the road. Some mornings, I saw him with one of my father-in-law's jumpers on to protect him against the cold. Often, I would see him sipping a cup of sweet, black coffee or supping a plate of soup in Vladimir's parents' house. Always, he refused to see a doctor, "who would poison him." Sometimes, he would shake my hand. Always, he would warn me not to give him any more of "those pills that almost killed him." When I drove past him on the road, I would wave and give him a wider berth than usual, just in case he reached for another stone.

I enjoyed the sense of community where we lived, and very much appreciated the general willingness to look after and take in waifs and strays. Such human kindness was crucial in the battle against suffering. However, there were times when I felt the Ecuadorian authorities overstepped the mark and took responsibility for my children, when it was not necessary for them to do so.

Swerving past Justo one day, I went to pick up Tamara from nursery as usual. Her teacher always sent her homework to do, which I thought to be ridiculous for a three-year-old. However, I went along with it, as at least it gave me an idea of what she was doing at nursery. (Tamara never remembered what she had done.) That day, there was a note in her book saying that the following day a doctor was going to examine all the children, and could I be there at ten o'clock to accompany her. I told her teacher I did not want Tamara to be examined by a doctor I did not know, and that she already had sufficient medical check-ups.

You can only imagine my horror when the next day I went to collect Tamara, only to be presented with a prescription from the doctor (who had by then gone on his way). Not only had he examined my child without my consent or presence, but he had also prescribed her medicine for allergies, because she had a runny nose. I was incensed.

"Tamara does not have allergies," I told Vladimir emphatically. "She is recovering from a cold, which her classmates gave her. That doctor had no right to prescribe her medicine. He doesn't know if she's already taking medicine or if she has allergies to certain medicines. Anyway, I made it quite clear to her teacher that I didn't want her seen by the doctor. I send her to nursery for the education, not for medical treatment."

"We'll go and speak to the director," Vladimir agreed, seeing me so upset.

The director was apologetic, although I was not convinced she understood why I was so irate, and said that it would not happen again. I continued to send Tamara to nursery, but the matter weighed on my mind. Once again, I questioned my wisdom in educating the girls in Ecuador, and my ability to protect them from harm.

CHAPTER 13

LIVING TODAY AND
INVESTING IN TOMORROW

Ecuadorians live for today. Few invest in tomorrow financially. When an opportunity arises, they drop whatever they had planned on doing, to grab it without a second thought. As I was confronted with the uncertainty of life day after relentless day, I too began to wake and give thanks for the simple gift of a new day to live. I sought wisdom for how much time I should spend preparing for the future, and how much I should concentrate on living today.

Vladimir had been working hard on the farm. It was a few kilometres outside the village, with a river running along its border, beautiful tall bamboo framing the perimeter, and it was filled with banana plants. Vladimir had cleared the four hectares of flat ground beside the river and built us a small house there. Our plan was to build a campsite on the surrounding ground for school, youth and church groups to be able to come and enjoy their camps and retreats. It was a beautiful, peaceful setting for people to take pleasure in, and we had lots of ideas of how to make it a place for fun, fellowship and refreshment.

Vladimir had already flattened, put in drainage, and sown grass on the essential football pitch. He had also planted hundreds of trees, palm trees and flowering bushes as borders. Several Saturdays, we had gone together to plant orange, lemon, grapefruit, avocado and cinnamon trees. The mesh "greenhouses" for the anthurium plants were now in production, and another attraction for future visitors to enjoy. Vladimir had built a cement ford through the river and put hundreds of truckloads of stone and sand from the river bed onto the track through the farm. He had dug a large fish pool and stocked it with tilapia fish so that visitors would be able to catch their own suppers. He had built a water supply for the house and campsite, by collecting water from a spring on the farm in a large cement tank. The water was pumped to another tank on top of the hill, and then came down to the house under pressure. The electricity had just been connected. The next phase was to build a toilet block and an adventure playground.

"The house is nearly ready for us to move in," Vladimir informed me one afternoon. "We just need to paint the walls inside."

"I can help with that," I offered. "I painted our current house myself."

The next Saturday, we went to the farm to paint, leaving the girls with their grandparents. It was very tranquil on the farm. As we painted, we were accompanied by shrill bird song and deep croaking of frogs. The wind rustled the leaves on the growing trees and the rushing river splashed over the ford in the distance. Out of the window, I spotted yellow, blue and red tropical birds and stopped to gaze. A humming-bird whirred briefly by the window before darting off to find a nectar-filled flower.

We had great fun painting together. It was marvellous to spend time together, just the two of us. As we had married and had Tamara in quick succession, time alone together had always been something of a luxury. We had chosen rustic colours to paint the kitchen and dining area. I loved painting the blocks in the kitchen individually in a patchwork of colours to create a brick effect. Vladimir painted our room a deep burgundy red, combined with white. It looked very cosy. The girls' room, we painted in pastel shades, making squares of different colours on the largest wall, as we had seen done on an interior decorating programme on the television. It looked fantastic: just right for little girls.

At the end of a hard day painting, we swam in the river, washing off the sweat and paint, and refreshing ourselves agreeably.

"Imagine living here and being able to swim every day," Vladimir exhaled in rapture.

"It's paradise," I was enthralled. "What a magnificent place to live."

"We're doing well with the painting. A couple more Saturdays and we can move in."

"Do you think we will feel a bit isolated?" I asked. "There are no neighbours in sight."

"The farm-workers will be here during the day, and you will be out at work in the mornings anyway. I think we will soon get used to it."

"I'm going to miss living next door to Mary," I realised. "She helps me so much with the girls. The girls will miss their playmates next-door too."

"You'll be able to go and visit often. They're not far away really and you have a car now."

"Yes, that's true. I guess it will just take a bit of getting used to at the beginning."

"Anyway, we need to sell our current house, so that we have the funds to develop the next phase of the campsite," Vladimir was practical as usual. "We should be living here to look after the farm. We'll be able to have animals, produce our own eggs and chickens, catch our own fish, eat the bananas, and become more self-sufficient."

"The girls will love having the space outside to roam and play," I agreed. "It's a wonderful environment to grow up in."

The following week I had a parents' meeting at the nursery, so I left the girls with their grandmother to have their shower and tea. The meeting was surprisingly brief. I found myself free, with no one expecting me home for another hour. I took the chance to nip down to the farm alone. I sat on the doorstep of our new house, and looked around me as the sun was setting red and fiery behind the hills in the distance. The insects were beginning to buzz and rattle as the evening began. I paused to think.

Life was a funny thing. Who would have thought, when I set off for Ecuador that I would end up married to an Ecuadorian, raising my children in a small Ecuadorian village, and investing all my worldly wealth in a farm. Was this move to the farm a good idea? The hope was that it would grow to sustain us now, and to provide for us in our old age. Some days, life seemed so fragile I wondered how we could ever think so far into the future. Maybe, we should just live for today. I was concerned about our isolation and lack of security on the farm. There was no one on hand to raise the alarm if thieves entered at night. Would the girls be happy here, or would they miss the company of the neighbours? Was it a good idea to be investing all I had in Ecuadorian soil? What would happen if I wanted to go back to the UK? Would Vladimir, with his antipathy towards the idea of living in the UK, ever be persuaded to go with me? Was I trapped here forever?

Suddenly, I realised my thoughts were spiralling into panicking about events that would probably never happen. I lifted my eyes to the stars, which were now beginning to twinkle in the night sky. I would take a day at a time and see where this next step on life's adventure took us. I was ready for the move.

Changes were afoot for others in the village too. Rumours abounded and gossip was quick to spread, so only hours after he had gone, the news reached me that Señora Maria's husband had run off with a young woman, who was said to be expecting his baby.

Señora Maria came to see me with her five youngest children. "Well, he has gone and abandoned us for good now," she complained. "Apparently, the woman had a few thousand dollars saved up. I don't think he'll show his face around these parts again."

"How are you going to manage?" I asked them, realising all they could do was to take it a day at a time.

"Our brother is living with us at the moment, and working on the banana lorries, so he is helping buy food," Jacqueline replied. "The sewing money helps too."

"We need money to pay for our school breakfasts and for our test papers this week," Aracely interrupted. "Can you help us with that?"

"Yes, I can give you that from your sponsor money," I replied. "You can take the rest of the bananas on that head over there as well, if you would like." I looked at the children and noticed that Jhon was not looking very well. "Is Jhon OK?" I asked. "He's looking under the weather."

"He's had a cough for a couple of weeks and fever," Señora Maria answered sadly. "I've been praying for him every day and getting him to pray, but it hasn't made him better."

"Let me give him some medicine," I insisted, frustrated she had not brought him along before this. "Give him this antibiotic and these tablets for the fever."

A couple of days later, Jhon was in hospital. His teacher at school had taken him to the emergency department of the public hospital. Jhon was on intravenous antibiotics for a week for his pneumonia. He could have died. His mother or sister tried to go and see him most days, but sometimes they did not have the bus fare, and other people were weary of always loaning them money that was never repaid. Ten-year-old Jhon had to endure being in that strange hospital all by himself. I wondered how he ever managed to stay in bed that long. He was normally such an irrepressible rogue. Perhaps the butch, armed security guard posted at the door of the ward scared him, or perhaps he was simply too sick to move.

I was glad when at last he came home again - thinner, pale and with blood shot eyes - but full of his usual cheek and mischief. The neighbours took his plight to heart and made sure he had good food while he was recovering. He soon returned to his usual tricks. People used to look at the children and say that they were hardy, that it did not matter that they went around without shoes or adequate clothing, dirty and hungry. They forgot about the three dead babies who had not made it. The truth was, these were the children who had survived so far, and they were vulnerable.

I had another issue to confront Señora Maria with. As a very low income family, they were entitled to receive a benefit from the government. Señora Maria was not claiming it.

"Señora Maria," I began, when she came again to ask for money. "Why are you not claiming the benefit the government offers you? You are in desperate need of money to feed your family. You should be claiming it."

"Our church says it is of the devil and forbids us to claim it," she told me. I wished I could give them a piece of my mind.

"And does this church of yours help you? Do they give you money?" I asked, knowing that on the contrary they asked her to give them money.

"No," she shook her head, looking at the floor, ashamed to admit it.

"So, if they aren't willing to help you, they have no right to tell you who you can or cannot take money from. You have no income. You have five children to feed. You need the money the government is offering you. I am going to be hard with you. If you don't go and claim that money, I'm not going to give you any more sponsor money either. Money does *not* come from the devil. It's God's provision for us. Now go and claim that money."

She began to claim the money and stopped hassling the neighbours for every little thing she needed.

Meanwhile, Señora Maria's daughter, Esther, had moved out of the shack in her garden. Steven had found a job on a farm, which included the loan of a house, so he and Esther had gone to live there. I was glad they had found better accommodation. They were living from day to day, counting the moments until their baby was born.

Esther went into labour, and Steven took her to the hospital on the bus. She was not progressing in labour, so they sent her home again. The next day, Steven took her back to the hospital, again on the bus, with increasing labour pains and the hospital said they were too full to attend to her. She had to go to a private clinic and pay for her delivery. Steven took her to the recommended clinic, where they told him she needed a caesarean section, but that they would not do the operation until he paid two hundred dollars. Steven did not have even twenty dollars, so he came to the health centre in search of Hortencia and me in a panic.

"Esther is there in so much pain and they say she can't give birth naturally. She's had pains for two days now. I need to pay for the caesarean and I don't have the money. Can you help me? I'll pay it back, I promise."

Whilst perhaps it would have been wiser to save for such an emergency, I knew that was a foreign concept to Ecuadoreans. They usually needed every penny they earned, and had just hoped that Esther would be attended to in the hospital, where they only had to pay for any medicines she was given. Esther was in a predicament. In Ecuador, women were not given any medicine for pain during labour. I could imagine Esther was exhausted after being in pain for such a long time. The baby was at risk now that it was such a prolonged labour. It seemed to me an awful thing that she was not receiving the operation she needed because they did not have the money to pay for it upfront. The baby might die. There were lives at stake.

Of course, I gave Steven the money and he rushed off shouting his thanks and promises of repayment. Esther gave birth to a healthy girl and was home the day after the operation, in a lot of pain. She came to Señora Maria's house, as it was the tradition for girls to be looked after for forty days after giving birth. Steven had to work, but came to see them with food whenever he could.

Esther was breastfeeding, as most Ecuadorians do. She could not afford to do anything else anyway. Unfortunately, she developed mastitis from a blocked duct. Her mother went and found a puppy dog and brought it to Esther for the puppy to suckle her breast to try and clear the stagnant milk that had accumulated. I was astonished at such goings on.

Either the puppy dog, or the massages and hot compresses that I recommended, worked. A breast abscess was avoided. Soon, Esther was managing well with Maria-Fernanda, and she went back to live on the farm with Steven. They continued to live from day to day, not knowing what tomorrow would bring.

Señora Maria continued to live from meal to meal, trying to scrape together enough food to feed her hungry brood. For me, living in the present meant choosing to read my girls another story, instead of working longer hours. It meant being willing to change my plans at a moment's notice, to attend a family birthday party or spontaneous gathering. It meant giving a helping hand when I was asked, not putting it off until tomorrow.

CHAPTER 14

TRANSFORMATION

The longer I lived in Ecuador, the more I became aware of my dependence on God for the daily blessings and protection I enjoyed. Frequently, amongst the suffering and the hardships, I also witnessed marvellous transformations. These signs of hope lit the way, inspiring faith in God despite the difficulties and sorrows.

For us, the next change was moving day. We borrowed a lorry from Fred and Mary next door, and piled in all our belongings. On the farm, we unloaded them and Vladimir set about rebuilding the furniture, while I put away the clothes and kitchen equipment. It was exciting to see our new home taking shape, and it was not long before every chair, bed and saucepan had a new place of residence.

The girls were pleased to see their trampoline in the garden, and a tree that they could climb. Emily was a bit upset by the move, and took a while to settle, but Tamara loved playing outside in the large open spaces and building sandcastles by the river.

Vladimir went and bought a crateful of forty chicks. Tamara and Emily helped him to set up their home in the henhouse, with a light bulb for warmth, food and water. Soon, we would have eggs and chickens to eat.

The girls also helped to feed the baby tilapia fish in the pool each day, and caught the tadpoles that swam by the edge. Day by day, we watched them grow legs, and lose their tails, as they transformed into frogs.

Big stripy caterpillars clung to the tall balsa wood trees. We watched the chrysalises form and the butterflies emerge. The miracle of transformation in nature was evident all around us. It reminded me daily of God's power to change our lives, situations and hearts. It gave me faith to believe this same miracle of transformation was possible in the lives of those around us.

Fiona came to join us on the farm. She (or should I say he) was a male turkey that belonged to Vladimir's sister. Sandy had thought Fiona was a female when a chick, hence had given him the name Fiona, which had stuck. Fiona was a fierce guard, ready to attack strangers with a vicious flick of her wings. His strutting and gobbling around our house soon became a familiar and welcome sound.

A florist client of Vladimir gave us two cocker spaniels, to keep us company and protect us. They were very tame, docile creatures, with stunning, red coats. They also barked wildly whenever anyone approached the house, giving us warning of their arrival. Dogs in Ecuador eat soup, so I learnt to cook for the dogs, as well as the family, every day.

Vladimir's parents killed some of their guinea pigs for a house-warming barbeque one evening. They came with the prepared creatures and roasted them on spits over the hot charcoal, turning them constantly, so that their skin crisped up deliciously, instead of burning.

As we munched the succulent meat, accompanied by boiled manioc and salad, we enjoyed the peaceful, beautiful surroundings of the farm and the good company of family. We talked about how best to build the adventure playground, and how to keep rabbits so that visiting children could pet them. It was good to dream and imagine.

Tamara and Emily were looking at a turtle Vladimir had found in the fish pool that afternoon. He had taken it out, so that it would not eat the fish, and had left it in a bucket for them to see.

"Did you know turtle blood is a certain cure for asthma?" Vladimir's Dad asked me. "It's a great remedy."

"Is it really?" I questioned, trying to hide my scepticism. "I think this poor turtle would rather we put him back in the river. I think I'll stick to the inhalers for my patients." I was well used to these bizarre remedies by then.

Vladimir took the girls and the turtle to the river, and set the turtle free, much to my relief. The girls were fascinated. They loved doing things with their Papi. I was content, as I watched everyone enjoying themselves. It was a delightful place to be.

* * *

Tamara was given another slip of paper at nursery saying that the doctor was going to visit the following day. This time, I did not send her to nursery that day, so that there was no chance she would be examined.

"Where was Tamara yesterday?" her teacher asked me.

"I didn't bring her, so that she wouldn't be seen by the doctor," I replied.

"Oh, that's a shame. The doctor didn't come yesterday, after all," her teacher informed me.

"When is he going to come?" I asked.

"I'm not sure. It might be today or tomorrow. Don't worry I'll make sure Tamara doesn't get seen this time," she assured me.

Frustrated by this typical example of the Ecuadorian's inability to stick to a plan, I left Tamara, hoping her teacher would keep her word, my protective instincts aroused.

Señora Maria did not want any harm to come to her children either, but trouble seemed to knock at her door. She sent Jacqueline, her sixteen-year-old daughter, to help Esther for a few days with the new baby. Jacqueline returned a couple of days later claiming that Steven had attempted to rape her. Señora Maria went to the Police, and Steven and Esther went into hiding. Nothing more was done about the case, and there was no way of knowing what the truth of the matter was. Steven lay low for a while, waiting for the storm to blow over. Esther could not come to the sewing group during this time, but needed the money more than ever, so she sent her work via Hortencia. I wondered how Esther felt. She vigorously denied Jacqueline's claims and stuck up for her partner. But then, if she didn't, who was going to take care of her and their little baby?

The psychologist from the school came to see me to ask about Señora Maria's family.

"The children come to school hungry. They don't have shoes for physical education. They fall asleep in class. They're often ill. They can't join in art classes, because they don't take the materials they need. Sometimes they don't go to school at all, because they don't have the bus fares. Can you help them at all?" she asked me.

"We've already built them a house," I began. "The community has given them drinking water on tap. I gave them all gym shoes at the start of the year, but they don't look after them. I give them medicines for free whenever they come to the health centre, but often they don't come when they are ill. Whenever they ask me for materials for school, I give them to them. I give them their bus fares every Monday. They each receive more than their sponsors give them, and more than other children in other families who are equally as poor. The girls are teenagers now. They need to help their mother by working when they are free."

"They are children still," the psychologist objected. "Children shouldn't work."

"Jacqueline is sixteen and Aracely is fifteen. I had weekend jobs at that age. Other young people living around here work and help their families as well as attending school. I already give them all I can. They need to help themselves as well."

I tried to encourage Jacqueline to look for work at the weekends, to help her mother. Señora Maria said Jacqueline was too traumatised and nervous to look for work. I could not help thinking the family had become too dependent. Perhaps, we helped them too much and they had come to expect other people to provide for them. I decided to offer Jacqueline the job of washing my car each Saturday, instead of giving more hand-outs. I felt she needed to start taking responsibility for herself and her family.

Jacqueline did come. She washed the car, and painted the gate, and earned a little money for herself. I hoped it would ignite a spark of initiative in her and give her the confidence to try doing other things to help herself as well.

Others in the sewing group were doing really well. Tania and her classmates Yadira, Angela, Roxana, Diana and Jenny were all in their last year of secondary school. Tania, who dear Don Claudio had feared would never marry, had in fact already found her Prince Charming and married him. She was studying her final year of school by distance learning: attending classes at the weekends and doing the coursework during the week at home. She was planning to sit her final exams a few weeks before her baby was due. She and her husband lived next door to her mum and Lorena. Tania, together with her other sisters, made sure that her mum had all she needed. Lorena, in turn, helped Tania with the sewing work.

Cousins Yadira, Angela and Roxana were talking about their plans to go to university with Jenny who made jewellery for Project Ecuador.

"We have to sit this new exam to get into university," Jenny explained to me. "The government has just brought it in this year. My Dad's saving up, to pay for a course that will prepare me for it."

"It's a national exam," Yadira continued. "Your results determine which course you will be offered at a state university. You might be offered a place in a completely different city though."

"Otherwise, we can apply for a place at a private university, and pay fees, but stay at home. If we go to a different city we would have to pay board and lodging," Roxana explained.

"What would you like to study girls?" I asked them.

"I would like to be a nurse," Yadira stated enthusiastically.

"I want to study administration, to do book keeping and that sort of office work," Jenny related.

"I want to study computing," Roxana announced.

"I would like to be an engineer," Angela asserted.

"We have three opportunities to sit the exam, to see if we can get enough points to study the subject we choose. If not, we'll have to settle for something else."

"You have all shown yourselves to be hard workers and very conscientious," I commended them. "Look how you have dedicated yourselves to sewing for six years now. Week after week, you have made beautiful goods, and brought them to me. You're all capable of doing well, whatever subject you end up studying. Just keep working hard, doing your best, and you'll find it pays off. With a university degree, you'll be able to get good jobs and never again fear being hungry. I'm very proud of each of you."

I was proud of them. Roxana and Angela's mother was the single mother of five girls. She worked her hands to the bone to provide for them. All her girls were hard-working, ambitious and respectful. It was a joy to have been able to give them a helping hand with their schooling and see them full of hopes and dreams for the future. Their lives had been transformed.

Another life was being transformed before our eyes, much to everyone's amazement and incredulity. Jessica's drug-trafficking father had started attending the local church, and had become a Christian. The transformation was truly incredible.

He stopped drinking alcohol completely, and renounced drugs and smoking. He stopped going on frequent trips to Colombia and stayed home – sober. We could not believe it. We were so used to seeing him drunk all the time.

"I can't remember the last time I saw Efren drunk," I remarked to Vladimir one day. "He really seems to be making an effort."

"Making an effort?" Vladimir retorted, "It's nothing short of a miracle. Only God could make such a change in someone's life. He was all that is bad and rotten, and now he has nothing to do with those vices at all. Did you know his first wife has taken him back?"

"No!" I exclaimed. "I didn't know he had a first wife."

"Oh yes. He abandoned her for Jessica's mother. He has three sons with his first wife. He left her alone to bring up the boys, while he lived with Jessica and her mother, and did not help her at all. Two of the boys are still at home. They're about eleven and twelve years old. Now that he is a changed man, and attending her church, she agreed to give him a second chance. He's living with them, and working in the fields, and paying the bills."

"That's amazing!" I paused to take in this astonishing news. "She's a brave woman. What about Jessica?"

"Efren and his wife want her to go and live with them now. I think my aunt is in agreement and that Jessica will move in soon."

I hoped the change would prove to be lasting, and that this truly could be a new start for all of them. I lost count of the number of people who I heard remarking that they had to believe in God if He could change Efren's life around like that. Everyone marvelled at the change in the man.

Efren started taking responsibility for Jessica's education. He came to thank me for helping her with a sponsor and gave me a sack of fresh oranges. Jessica was growing taller and more confident. She grew close to her step-mother and blossomed under her care.

When Hortencia and I went to test the vision of all the children in the local primary school, we discovered Jessica could not see clearly. We took all those who could not see perfectly to an optician in town, to be tested for glasses. I used charity funds to purchase glasses for those who needed them. The optician did give Jessica glasses, but took me aside and told me she thought the problem was more psychological. Knowing Jessica's background I was not surprised.

I spoke to Efren and asked him if he had considered taking Jessica to see a psychologist.

"I would love to give her that help, Doctor, but I can't afford to pay for it. Psychologists tend to be expensive," he admitted.

"I'm sure the psychologist in Orphaids would help her, without charging you anything," I offered. "If I arrange an appointment for you, will you take Jessica?"

"Oh yes, Doctor," Efren appeared genuinely grateful. "I will certainly take her."

So I arranged an appointment for Jessica, and Efren did take her to the psychologist several times. He really was trying to do the best for his family now, in stark contrast to his past. God's grace and mercy was evident to all.

CHAPTER 15

GRACE AT WORK

I could see faith-inspiring grace at work in other situations in the community as well. Martha, a deaf and dumb single mum of two gorgeous girls, was in the sewing group. She asked me to go with her to visit her uncle, who was dying of gastric cancer. We bumped our way along an unmade road for forty-five minutes, in order to get to his house. Clouds of dust lay in our wake. Finally, the little cottage appeared on the horizon, surrounded by green fields.

Gilberto was in his fifties. He was skeletally thin, lying in bed moaning. He did not open his eyes: he was in so much pain. He had a bad reputation as a man who had drunk away his family's money. He had sold their cattle to pay for his addiction. His wife and grown-up children were left with a house and nothing more. They had all suffered at his hands. The neighbours whispered, saying it served him right to have cancer, that it was God's punishment on him for the way he had wasted his life. His family were grace itself.

Gilberto's wife was a gentle, Christian woman. I did not know all she had suffered in her marriage and family life, but I knew her husband had not made things easy for her. Yet, when I went to their house there was no reproach in her voice. She was a tender nurse. She was anxious to alleviate her husband's pain.

"Gilberto's in so much pain," she began. "Can you give him something so that he does not suffer so? He's also vomiting a lot and very constipated. I hate to see him like this. There must be something we can do."

"Yes, of course," I replied putting a patch on his skin to alleviate the pain and giving an injection for the vomiting. "We must do everything we can to make Gilberto feel comfortable."

His wife smiled at me gratefully. "In the hospital they just sent him home saying there was nothing more they could do. But there are medicines that can help aren't there?"

"Yes, he's going to feel much more comfortable very soon," I promised, touched by her concern. "I'll come back in a day or two and see how he's doing. You just make sure you give him all the medicines as I have told you to."

A few days later I did return, and this time Gilberto himself greeted me, with a warm hand shake and smile. His pain was now controlled and he was a different man. He was still too weak to get out of bed, but he could now cooperate and converse. Being able to help patients like this was what kept me in Ecuador. Gilberto and his family were profoundly thankful.

"Thank you Doctor for these medicines," he breathed. "They are helping me enormously. I was in mortal agony and just wanted to die. Now, I can enjoy the days God grants me with my family. I am so thankful to my wife and daughters for all they're doing for me.

It's a blessing to have these last days with them. God is merciful."

Gilberto's wife was thrilled with the change in him. As we walked down the garden path together to the car, she chatted about Gilberto.

"This is a very precious time for us, Doctor. Gilberto has done many things he shouldn't have done, but now he's had the chance to ask our forgiveness and to tell us how sorry he is. I thank the Lord for sending you to us to help him. I don't know how long he has left in this world, but I want you to know how important these days are for us." The bone-shaking ride home was made worthwhile by these heart-felt words.

Tamara turned four and wanted a "proper" birthday party. I think seeing the suffering, depravity and poverty around me every day made celebrating life, and all that is good, more important to me. Ecuadorians often have a special party for their baby when they reach one year. I guess the tradition came about because many babies do not make it to their first birthday, so it is a special milestone. In the same way, my awareness of the fragility of life, and the closeness of death, made me appreciate the wonder of life more. I wanted Tamara to have a birthday she would not forget and to feel like a princess in the process. She was one very excited little girl.

I cut up the dress I wore for our wedding blessing to make her a princess dress for the party. It was long and floated and sparkled and Tamara loved it. I enlisted help to cook up a big tea, and we invited all the little cousins and neighbourhood friends. When the children gathered, we played lots of games in the garden, amidst much laughter and many squeals. Vladimir's sister had brought enchanted pots for the children. We hung up the clay pots, and then lined up the children. One by one, they were blindfolded and had to hit the pot with a stick three times. If they broke it they could have the sweets that fell from its inside. The children loved having a go. Then, we hung up the large, pink princess piñata. All the children gathered excitedly underneath it as Vladimir pulled out the bottom. Sweets, chocolates and little toys fell to the ground as the children scrambled to pick up as many as they could. It was mayhem and Tamara's favourite game.

Vladimir's family had created an archway of pink balloons, which stood at the end of the garden next to the table with the birthday cake. Tamara posed there with her friends for photos, before we all sang "Happy Birthday" to her at the tops of our voices. Tamara smiled and smiled. She was having a wonderful time.

Before we served the tea, Vladimir's Uncle said grace. "Heaven Father, we thank you for another day of life and for another year of life for Tamara. We thank you for the gift of unity: that we can gather as a family today to celebrate this special little girl. We thank you for the food you give us each day and for this meal we are about to enjoy. Amen." The prayer summed up what was in my heart also.

We busied ourselves serving the meal, and everyone tucked in gratefully. Some food was stowed in plastic bags for the recipients to take home. This would be given to family members who had not come to the party. There were no left-overs.

After everyone had eaten their fill of tea, we handed out the goody-bags, and the children took their leave. Tamara ran inside excitedly to open her presents. It was wonderful to see her so happy. I was glad we had given her a very special day in honour of the gift of another year of life.

Tamara went into reception year at school and I began to teach her to read English at home. This had always been my plan. I figured they would teach her to read Spanish at school, but I wanted to make sure that, as well as speaking English she learnt to read and to write it too. I was a little nervous she would find it difficult because English is not phonetic like Spanish, so I wanted to get started straight away teaching her the letter sounds and sight words in English.

Tamara had always enjoyed books, stickers and drawing, so she naturally started trying to write the letters she found in the Peppa Pig magazines her Granny sent her from Scotland. They were not teaching them how to form letters at school yet, so I did, to make sure she learnt to form them correctly.

I had imagined I could leave maths to the school, but discovered she was not yet doing much in the way of numbers and logic. I wanted her to be at the level her peers were in the UK, so I started playing maths games with her in the afternoons as well.

I wondered how we would get on as she progressed through school. I went to visit friends who had eight-year-olds in school, and compared what they were doing with the kind of maths children would be doing in the UK. I could see that if I left her in an Ecuadorian school, I was going to have to supplement her work, but thought it would be possible. I imagined she could attend school in the morning and then do extra English and Maths with me in the afternoons. I hoped it would work out, because there were not many alternatives, unless we were to move city to be near an International School. I still felt I had plenty of work to do in Santo Domingo, and then there was the farm/campsite project to consider as well. Doubts continued to niggle in my mind, but I decided to persevere for the time being.

Living on a farm, Tamara and Emily were learning new things every day. They witnessed nature on their doorstep. They were learning how to look after chickens and fish, how to plant seeds and look after plants. I was proud the day Tamara swam across the river without her armbands, and loved to watch the lines of marching ants with Emily. The girls wandered in and out of my consulting room some days, and asked questions about the wounds they saw. They accompanied us when we went visiting and always asked "why?"

We went to visit the Martinez family. They were living in our village in a slum area. This meant the families there had gone and taken the plots without permission. Since then, the local council had given them papers for their plots. The families living there were all very poor.

The Martinez family lived on one such plot. Their house was made of bits of wood and tottered on stilts. It was just one room, which measured about three metres by three metres. The parents and two children all cooked, ate and slept in that one room.

When we went in, Tamara was full of questions. "Why do they have such a small house Mummy? Why don't they have glass in the windows? Why don't they have any toys to play with?"

"They are very poor Tamara," I explained. "Their Papi didn't go to school much, so he can't get a good job. He doesn't have much money, so they can't build a nice house or buy toys for their children."

Tamara needed the toilet. They didn't have one. As she relieved herself on the ground outside, she asked why they did not have a lavatory. She was learning all about poverty and how privileged she was. I hoped such experiences would spark in her too a sense of gratitude for life and its blessings. I hoped she and Emily would grow up thankful, generous girls.

We went to visit the Martinez family to consider them for the building project. Each year, we received funds to build houses for local families, and Vladimir and his team did the honours. It would be wonderful to be able to give this little family a proper dwelling that was safe and dry, with a hygienic toilet and shower. Friends were raising funds in the UK and we hoped there would be enough to build this family a house of their own. The transformation would be incredible. We would build them a house with two bedrooms, a bathroom and a kitchen/dining room. They would be safe and secure and protected from the elements. To them it would seem like a palace. It was a wonderful gift to be able to give a family – an expression of God's grace.

CHAPTER 16

THANK YOU FOR ANOTHER DAY OF LIFE

I arrived home from a visit to Piedad. Her face was even more swollen, and the tumour had now eaten away a hole in the roof of her mouth, making it difficult for her to eat. Despite the grotesque growth, which had stolen her beauty and her dignity, she remained very positive as she confronted life. Her "good morning" was made with a lopsided smile. Her eyes shone, as she saw she was remembered by us. She hesitated to complain, preferring to gossip proudly about her grandchildren and the wonderful progress they were making in life. She showed us a photograph of herself with her late husband when she had been unblemished and beautiful, and reminisced about her adventures bringing up eight children on a farm. As she talked with us, she constantly dabbed at the dripping wound on her face, and turned her head to hear our replies, as the tumour had made her deaf in one ear. Her inner beauty did not cease to shine through her damaged outside. She made me feel very humble.

"We should give thanks every day for the gifts of life and health," I remarked to Vladimir. "I love the way

Ecuadorians generally start their prayers with thanks for the simple gift of another day of life. I just take it for granted, to tell the truth. It doesn't seem to matter how many times I visit brave people like Piedad and Gilberto, who are coming to the end of their days before their time, I still forget this important lesson. Instead of pausing at the start of each day to thank God for the new opportunity to love and be loved, I rush into the day. Before I realise it, I am worrying about getting the girls out of the door on time, what we are going to have for lunch, and a thousand other insignificant details. I would love to live life under a blanket of thankfulness, enveloped, entwined and immersed in gratitude. I don't want to take these most wonderful blessings of health, family, and life itself for granted. I want to celebrate them every day. There is great meaning in so many small moments: moments I usually fail to even notice. I'm just too busy thinking about the next thing on my list."

"Wow," Vladimir joked, "you have been impacted by these patients of yours. It is true what you say though. Each new day is a gift from the hands of God who made us, and knows our beginning and our end. Our lives are in His hands. Each new day is a day to be lived to the full."

"When I take it for granted that I should live to be eighty or more, and enjoy good health all my days, then I am shocked and disturbed when tragedy occurs. The truth is we are in the midst of a war between good and evil. I should expect bad things to happen to rich and poor alike, to the good and to the bad. I too cause pain to others sometimes, through my words and actions. I don't deserve to have a pain-free life. It's the grace of God that grants me each day of health, each moment of joy, and each experience of love. I hope that when the bad days come, when I am in the midst of pain and in the shadow of death, I have the humility to receive His help and strength, not rebuke Him for allowing me to suffer."

"I have great admiration for those who endure the long suffering illnesses such as cancer bring," Vladimir reflected. "Yet the desire to live is so strong. Even in the midst of great pain many people still hope to live another day."

"The hope of heaven keeps me going. One day we'll be at home with Jesus, with everyone living in complete harmony and love. I believe good will triumph over evil in the end. I believe Jesus has won that victory. That makes it worth fighting now."

As we continued the fight, we were privileged to witness heaven breaking through to earth, examples of God's love touching hearts. Nancy was a mother with young children. She had terminal cancer. She lived in great poverty. Her house, if you could call it that, was built on a now abandoned rubbish dump. She had very few resources with which to confront cancer. She did not have money and she did not have an education. She did not know much about her illness or how it could be treated effectively. She did not have anyone to take her to appointments or accompany her to Quito to the hospital. She was alone. That is until the "Life in Abundance" Christian charity workers took her under their wing and fought her corner for her.

These Christians were love in action. They prayed for her and with her, but they also took her to appointments and bought her medicine. They took her to Quito to the cancer hospital, and then to another when the hospital would not receive her. They gave the children food and medicines. Nothing was too much trouble for them. They showed Nancy the love of Jesus, and Nancy wanted to know that love for herself.

One afternoon, her friends brought her to the river on our farm. She sat on a plastic chair, her feet in the water as they sang hymns of thankfulness to God. The Pastor read words of love and comfort from the Bible and then baptised her, pouring water from the river over her head.

Tamara and Emily splashed beside me in the shallows, their laughter intermingling with the singing and prayers. They were unaware of the significance of Nancy's witness, but accepted her children as playmates in the river without question. Those children lost their mother a couple of weeks later. She went to be with her Saviour. She died knowing that she was no longer alone and that her children were not alone either. Her eldest daughter took on their care, with the on-going support of "Life in Abundance" workers.

Hortencia and I were worried by the nauseating smell emanating from the waiting room in the health centre. We quickly wheeled in Don Dueñas so that the other patients did not have to suffer the stench.

"I just want to know if there is any hope for my foot or not," was his opening gambit. "The butchers at the hospital want to cut off my leg. I would rather die. I agreed to come here as our last resort. If you say you can heal it, I will do as you say."

Don Dueñas' wife looked embarrassed at her husband's abrupt approach and chimed in more gently.

"He has diabetes. He stood on a nail and his foot became infected. The hospital says it is hopeless and that if they don't amputate he will get gangrene and die. We heard you might be able to help." She looked at us, asking the question with her eyes.

Hortencia calmly removed the pus-filled, stinking gauze and gently bathed the foot. It was a ball of rotting flesh, terribly swollen, red and purple and nauseating. Don Dueñas' wife could not bear the odour and left the room.

Don Dueñas could not feel his foot, so I cut away dead tissue ruthlessly, exposing the tendons and putrefying muscles, cleaning away the pus. It was certainly a worse case than I had treated before, but there was no gangrene and the foot had circulation. So I decided to give the foot a chance. After all, there was nothing to lose.

Hortencia enveloped the huge wound with honey and gauze, while I wrote a prescription for antibiotics. We sent Don Dueñas on his way with no promises, but with hope. He came every day for a dressing change. Hortencia spent hours cleaning and dressing his ulcer. She had never gone to secondary school, but she had a gentle hand, a quick eye, great patience and a disarmingly kind manner. She paid no attention to Don Dueñas' grumpiness and pessimism. She faithfully dressed that foot every day, even though at first it seemed a thankless task. God was at work in her patience and perseverance. Victory was found in faith and hope.

After two weeks, no one could deny that the smell was less, the wound was cleaner and that new flesh was beginning to grow. Those tentacles of beautiful red flesh began to bubble and spread, covering the tendons and muscles that had been laid bare. I watched astounded, as the wound filled in. Don Dueñas wife, who at first could not even look at the wound, started doing dressings herself at home some days. Her eyes reflected the renewed hope she was experiencing.

Don Dueñas was ever his grumpy self: reluctant to swallow tablets and not compliant with his diet. However, as he felt better and began to see the difference in his foot, he started talking about taking photographic evidence to those who had wanted to chop off his limb. He recovered his ebullient spirit and took an interest in those around him again. His face lost its grey, drawn look and his eyes regained their spark.

I was glad we were winning this battle. Don Dueñas was precious: precious to God. The moments we shared together while dressing his foot, were times we spent fighting for good, for life and health. He was worth fighting for. I never ceased to wonder at the human body's amazing potential to heal. Witnessing the growth of flesh in Don Dueñas foot was a parable of the healing and renewal God can bring us in so many different circumstances and different ways. It was inspiring. It gave me faith to seek the hand of God at work in other more complex situations. It gave me the faith to seek His wisdom in how to resolve my ever growing misgivings over Tamara's education.

CHAPTER 17

THE HOPE OF HEAVEN

I was surprised to see Esther, Steven and baby Fernanda by the road side in the village, waiting for the bus. It seemed that they had now come out of hiding. Was all forgiven and forgotten?

I discovered that they were back living in the tiny board room at the back of Señora Maria's house. Jacqueline and her brothers and sisters helped to care for their niece Fernanda with enthusiasm, and hugged and kissed their sister Esther as though there had never been a cross word between them. The police were forgotten. Steven was looking for work again and doing casual labour in the fields in the meantime. Between them all, they had something to eat each day. The fight for survival took precedence over the rights and wrongs of what had gone before.

Tamara never usually told me about anything she did at school. Every day I asked her, "What did you do today dear?" Every day she responded with a puzzled frown and a shrug. She was already on to enjoying the next

149

event of the day and had no time for reflecting on what was in the past.

One night, however, she started to giggle at a sudden memory. "Mummy," she laughed, "do you know what my English teacher said today? She said *treeanglay* instead of triangle. Wasn't that funny?" Tamara rolled about laughing and I could not help grinning myself. Seeing my amusement Tamara started recollecting, and inventing, all kinds of other bad pronunciations of English words as we enjoyed the joke together.

Another evening, Tamara suddenly asked me, "Mummy, why do they teach me things I already know at school?"

"What kind of things?" I asked her, interested by this little window which had opened into her world.

"Oh, the colours, the shapes, the numbers, English." Tamara reeled off her little list in a bored fashion. "I already know these things."

"You know Tamara that is a very good question actually." I gave her a kiss on her forehead as she turned over to sleep and I asked myself the same question.

Christmastime was approaching. Families and shops set up nativity scenes. Looking at the baby Jesus figures, my thoughts turned to the Jesus who died and rose again. My thoughts turned to the promise of new life and eternity. Lifting my gaze from problems and pain, I focused instead on joy and peace. Seen in the light of the suffering around me, heavenly realities appeared clearer.

Christmas was an opportunity to celebrate the blessing of family, and Vladimir's family were determined to celebrate in style. All year, each family unit had saved up ten dollars a month so that there was a fund available to pay for a Christmas weekend together on our farm. Vladimir's mother had three siblings. Each of them with their spouse, children and grandchildren gathered on the farm on the Saturday morning to eat *encebollado*, which is a delicious fish soup. My sister Rachel and her husband Adam were visiting us, and were made very welcome. There were about fifty of us in total.

The preparations had been thorough. The farm was decorated with balloons and a banner welcoming everyone. Vladimir had dragged Adam on to the football pitch in the dark to measure out the markings with his laser. The football match was taken very seriously. Games had been organised and of course the food: food in abundance and overflowing, mouth-watering, delectable and varied. Uncle Roman's pig had been slaughtered for the occasion.

The family was divided into two teams. We were in the blue team and all had a blue T-shirt. Those who had travelled from the border town of Machala were the red team and all wore red T-shirts.

After the breakfast, where everyone was greeting each other and catching up on family news, the games began in earnest. First, each team lined up in formation to present their *Madrina*: the woman dressed up to be the team beauty queen. The formal welcome and introduction given, Vladimir's mother won the draw to be Madrina of the games, and we all whooped and danced as she was presented with a bouquet of exotic flowers, beautifully arranged in a large pink bow.

I was first to compete for my team in the swimming-across-the-river stint of the relay race. Next up was a cousin who ran to the football pitch. Here, a couple took over in a piggy-back sprint, followed by Vladimir downing a baby bottle full of fizzy drink. By the time the relay reached its last contestants, the cries of "cheat" abounded as they accused each other of biting a larger hole in the teat. We roared with delight as Vladimir finished first and jumped around claiming points for our team.

Everyone had to participate in the games. The boys were hilarious swinging a banana suspended on a piece of string between their legs to hit a ball. All the couples joined in throwing an egg back and forth until it broke. The visitors were made to put Vaseline on their noses and move cotton wool balls between basins. Then, the husbands were blindfolded and challenged to identify their partners by touching the hands of the line of wives. (Vladimir identified my hand correctly, much to his relief!)

At the end, the points won were added up to see who was in the lead. We jumped and cheered to find the blue team were winning. The football match still remained to be played.

For the guys, all avid football players (one was even a professional), this was the highlight of the day. The match was played out in earnest, as the men passed, tackled and shot at goal. The result was a victory for the reds and we all gathered nervously to see who would be the overall winner for the day. A cheer erupted from the blues as we pipped the reds at the post and lined up to receive our medals. Everyone was happy and ready for lunch.

Lunch was a huge barbeque of all things pig. There were ribs and pieces of leg, the intestines stuffed with the minced organs to make sausages, the skin and the fat. The toasted ears and tails had been eaten by the cooks already. The succulent pork was served with boiled maize and barbequed yellow plantain bananas. I was very hungry and it was delicious. Everyone laughed and ate and shared and teased, until they had enjoyed their fill and more. The chat flowed on into the mid-afternoon, while the children happily played their own games around us, and then swam in the river.

Suddenly, Auntie Sandy clapped her hands and rounded us all up for the children's games. The children hopped and danced around excitedly, as they gathered together for their enchanted pots. These were strung up on a string and the children took turns to hit them until their treats spilled out on to the ground.

The secret Santa followed. Each of us had been allocated someone to buy a gift for beforehand. The gifts were given with kisses and hugs, and opened with great anticipation of the clothes and shoes inside.

Everyone groaned when the evening meal was announced. We were still full from lunchtime. The chicken soup was nonetheless dished up and handed round. It was scrumptious. It was very simple, made from corn-fed, free-range chicken and boiled banana. Yet, it was full of flavour. The children were ready for another meal, but the rest of us struggled to fit it in.

The evening stretched out as we conversed, laughed and ate ice-cream. It was warm, so we all happily sat outside enjoying the breeze.

"It certainly is different to a cold Christmas in Britain!" I commented to my sister.

"Yes, a lovely change," she remarked.

"It is nice," I agreed, "but I don't think it feels Christmassy. No matter how many twinkly lights there are, or how many Christmas carols I play, it just doesn't feel like Christmas. It is nonetheless fun!"

"I think this is how Christmas should be," Adam joined in. "Look at the whole family together, playing crazy games and having a wonderful time. This is what Christmas is all about. I'm having a fabulous time."

"I am too," Rachel agreed. "I don't miss the cold and the rain. It's incredible to be able to sit outside in the heat at Christmas. It's been an amazing day. It's good to make time to celebrate with family."

The festivities continued the next day with a breakfast of *empanadas:* banana pastry filled with cheese and fried. Those who wanted to played volleyball, while others relaxed until midday, when it was time for those who had several hours journey ahead of them to depart. With work and school the following day, they could not leave too late.

Only the 25th December and the 1st January were officially public holidays in Ecuador. Schools continued their classes and people had to go to work over the festive season. The community organised a Christmas party on the afternoon of the 24th December for all the village children. It was a chance for everyone to work together for the heavenly ideals of unity and love.

A month beforehand, a committee, including Vladimir and myself, had written about one hundred letters to different members of the community asking for contributions to make up bags of sweets and chocolates for the two hundred children. We hand-delivered the letters, and soon the contributions had been delivered to the health centre in dribs and dabs. The girls from the sewing group came to help pack the bags the day before the party. We made up four hundred bags: enough for all the children and most of the adults. It was a marathon operation, and Rachel and Adam did a great job tying the bags and curling the ribbons.

On the day, Hortencia organised a group of mothers to cook enough rice with chicken for the two hundred children. Another group of volunteers went to town to buy bread rolls to accompany hot chocolate for the adults. The local milkman donated the milk. Two of the older girls from the village dressed up as rag dolls to compere the games. Everyone participated and had great fun.

The children raced and jumped and sang in the competitions, winning toys as prizes. They were very happy. The final game was the Christmas Princess competition. The girls had to line up and model up and down, greeting the crowd and blowing kisses. Tamara joined in with great gusto, wiggling her hips with the best of them, and won the Princess sash and crown. She was delighted and raced up to give me a twirl. I laughed at my Ecuadorian girl.

The children ate their rice and chicken hungrily, asking for more. Then, there was a slice of cake, lovingly made by our friend Mary. It was good to see everyone, rich or poor all had something to eat that Christmas. We had made a Christmas appeal in the UK and raised funds to give out gifts to each of the children, along with their bag of sweets. The sewing group had made pirate and princess dressing up hats, handbags decorated with cats and draw-string bags. Rachel and Adam eagerly helped to hand out the presents to the excited children. The afternoon was full of smiles and happiness. Jacqueline was there with her siblings, all eating hungrily. Fatherless Tania and Lorena were sitting on the grass with the older girls, sipping hot chocolate and nibbling their bread roll as they laughed together. Motherless Jessica was munching her cake with her cousins, her step-mum not far from her side. As I looked around the thronging crowd in the village park, I could spot many patients, children with sponsors, a few we had built a house for, and the sewing ladies. I knew many of them faced large problems and obstacles. Some were recently bereaved. Others were fighting ill health. Today was a day to come together as a community to celebrate all that was good. It was a day that reminded us of the strength there was in working together and the support available in one another to fight the battle that life could be.

"I'm so glad you could be here with us today," I said warmly to Rachel and Adam. "You do so much for the charity - it is great you can witness for yourselves the joy and blessing it is to so many people. None of this would be possible without you and the others who support us at home."

"It's amazing to be here," Adam replied with his usual enthusiasm. "It's so different to our Christmas at home. We love sharing this with you."

CHAPTER 18

OUR KIND AND COMPASSIONATE GOD

Taking advantage of Rachel and Adam's visit, we took a few days holiday and headed off to the eastern jungles. Squeezing into the pick-up truck together, we travelled up the hair-raising Andes mountain road and down the other side to a small town called Baños. It was one of my favourite places in Ecuador. Set in the foothills of the Andes Mountains, its climate was temperate: neither too hot nor too cold. It was full of activities for tourists to do and rested in the most beautiful setting. The volcano Tunguragua towered over the town majestically, showering it in ash every now and then, as it had been active for the past few years. The town boasted of its thermal baths heated by the naturally hot springs.

Heading down the mountain side, there was a string of waterfalls, which cascaded in great elegance and power to the valley below. After resting a night in Baños, we set off to explore the waterfalls. The locals had zip wires stretched over the ravine and we were up for the thrill. Attached by the harness to the wire, we zoomed over the waterfall in turn, experiencing the adrenaline rush.

I took the girls across in the little rickety cable car, which seemed more dangerous than the zip wire. They stared large-eyed as the little car rushed across the ravine, rattling and squeaking. It was fun to see their reactions to these new adventures. The waterfalls glinted and sparkled in rainbow hues, illuminating the emerald green mountains. Small yellow, green and blue parrots flew among the trees. The sound of rushing water and bird-song was our sound-track. The moment was magical.

After the waterfall tour, we carried on our journey to the town of Puyo on the edge of the Amazon jungle. We went in a canoe down the river to visit an indigenous community. It was incredible to be gliding through the thick rainforest, watching the green trees rush by on either side. The local people danced and showed us their local traditions, while Tamara joined in the football game with the local children. We then climbed back into the canoe and went on to a small animal sanctuary.

"Wow, Mummy, look at the monkey!" Tamara cried. "It's jumping from branch to branch."

"I hope it doesn't bite me like that monkey did when we took Granny to the zoo!" Vladimir exclaimed keeping his distance.

"Look at the turtles in the pool," I pointed them out to Emily. "They're so big!"

"And see the caiman over there?" Vladimir showed us the small crocodile.

"Ooo, that's scary!" Tamara opened her eyes wide.

A little girl came up to us with a brightly coloured parrot sitting on a stick. She held it out to Tamara, who reached out to hold the stick with her. We snapped photos and then had a turn.

The tour over, we went back to the town in the canoe and bought snacks on the shore. "Careful the monkeys don't steal your food," the lady selling the corn-on-the-cobs warned us. As we looked over our shoulders, sure enough we noticed a host of monkeys watching us, their eyes sparkling greedily. Some of the monkeys had tiny babies on their backs. Tamara was enthralled. We stayed photographing them and enjoying the spectacle for a long while, until the setting sun forced us to find our hostel. The day had been a kaleidoscope of new images, smells and experiences.

"You know, I think Tamara has learnt more by visiting this incredible place than she has this entire term in school. It's so powerful being able to experience this for yourself, isn't it?" I commented to Rachel.

She gave me a quick hug. "It has been a wonderful trip," she concluded.

The visitors returned home, leaving a huge hole in my heart. Being apart from my family was the hardest part of living so far from home. Life returned to its usual routines and settled back to normal. Tamara was finishing her reception year at school. I was busy in the health centre and Emily was inventing imaginative stories with her dollies day by day. Vladimir was working on the farm, fertilising the flowers in anticipation of Valentine's day sales, and building the toilet block on the campsite.

At school, they were holding elections to vote in the student president. Tamara came home with an identity card she had made, and posters went up all around the school with photographs of the smiling candidates. I thought it was a reasonable exercise, until one day Tamara came out of school clutching a pretty little butterfly notebook with "List A" written on the back cover, and sucking a lollypop.

"Mummy, look at this beautiful book the big girl gave me," Tamara exclaimed happily, caressing the pretty picture.

"Who gave you the lollypop?" I asked sternly.

"Another big girl gave it to me. I'm telling the truth, Mummy. They want us to vote for them."

"They're teaching the children bribery and corruption at that school!" I exclaimed to Vladimir when we arrived home. "No wonder the country is full of corruption if this is the way they teach the children." When I showed him Tamara's notebook, Vladimir smiled.

"It's just a game really isn't it," he joked. "They're only children. Tamara doesn't even understand what a vote is."

"But that's the whole point! If they want to teach her what voting and an election is all about then they should have the candidates tell the children what they will do for the students, not give them bribes. If they're not old enough to understand, then it would be better not to do it at all!" I sighed frustrated.

"You take everything so seriously," Vladimir shrugged. "How did you get on in the health centre this morning?"

"It went very well thanks. Don Dueñas came for his foot to be dressed. It's a miracle how much better that foot is. He walked in today. He no longer needs a wheelchair. Isn't that fantastic? And I heard him talking to other patients in the waiting room who also have leg ulcers. He was telling them to have faith and that they would get better. He carries a little album of photos around with him. He has photos of his foot when it was at its worst, and up-to-date photos of how it is now. I have more patients because of him. When I spoke to the pharmacist in town the other day he said he knows Don Dueñas as well. He said he couldn't believe the difference in Don Duenas's foot. He too is recommending me to other patients."

"You're being kept busy then!"

"How are you getting on with the flowers?" I enquired.

"There will be a good number to cut for Valentine's day. My mum and aunt are coming to help cut and pack them for the next two days. Then I'll take them up to Quito to sell."

"Do go carefully, won't you," I worried. "It's raining so hard, now we are in the midst of the rainy season. You could get caught in a landslide or rain-storm."

"I'll be careful," Vladimir promised. "I heard that some of the girls you've helped are going to graduate from secondary school soon."

"Yes. It's so exciting!" I responded happily, "There are seven of them: Tania, Jenny, Angela, Yadira, Roxana, Diana and Gabi. Project Ecuador has helped them all the whole six years of secondary school. They are real Project Ecuador graduates!"

"It's definitely something to celebrate. It's a wonderful thing you have done. These girls wouldn't have been able to study without that help. It makes such a difference in their lives, especially as they are girls. Without education, there are no jobs for them. Now, they can defend themselves in life and make something of themselves. You should take them out to celebrate," Vladimir suggested.

"That's a very good idea," I agreed. "They really have overcome great obstacles to get this far. Gabi's father is quadriplegic and bed-bound. When I first met her in her house in the back of beyond, she was not attending school. She has done the whole six years by distance learning and faithfully helped her mother to care for her father as well. She's an inspiration. Jenny's father did not see the point in educating girls. She came to me with jewellery she had made, when she was twelve years old, to ask me if I would sell it for her on a regular basis, so that she could pay her own way through school. She kept at it for the whole six years and now she is graduating with a job in an office lined up. What a star! That girl's initiative will take her far. Roxana was born with a heart defect and has mild learning difficulties, but, boy, does she have determination. She failed three school years along the way, but repeated them and continued to study every hour God gave her, and now, aged twenty, has finished high school. Good for her! Yadira asked me if she could sew when she was twelve years old, because her father abandoned her when she was a baby and her mother did not have the money to pay for school. Yadira has had the support of a sponsor and has sewn faithfully the whole six years of school. She helps her mum with her little brother and is such a gentle, generous soul. I hope she does become a nurse, because she would be a good one. That's not to mention Angela, Diana and fatherless Tania who is about to become a mother. Look, just talking about them brings tears to my eyes. I'm so very proud of them. I will organise a meal out for them."

Vladimir smiled at my enthusiasm and gave me a quick hug. Emily came toddling up holding out her dolly for me to hold. I looked at her adorable, cute face and lifted her up too for a cuddle.

"What will become of our own daughters?" I asked Vladimir. "What will they want to do in life?"

"Maybe become a doctor like their Mummy?" Vladimir suggested, giving Emily a big kiss.

"Or maybe become an engineer like their Papi?" I proposed.

"Who knows what the future holds?"

I wanted to give them the opportunity to do whatever it was they chose in the future. How was I going to manage that in Santo Domingo?

Vladimir went to Quito to sell the flowers and did not make it home that night. He was half-way down the mountain in a tropical storm when he phoned me. "The road is blocked by a landslide. It's raining too hard for the diggers to be able to clear it tonight. I will have to stay the night in the nearest village and come down in the morning when the road opens," he told me.

Hardly able to hear him above the noise of the torrential rain I replied, "Just keep safe and come as soon as you can. We're all okay at home."

It was midday before he finally made it, tired, but none the worse for his adventure.

A couple of weeks later, I drove through the village collecting the seven elegant young ladies who were to accompany me for a celebratory meal. They all climbed into the truck, somewhat shy, and we headed off into town. I took them to a favourite restaurant of mine, which prepared mouth-watering grills, and we sat down to share the good food together.

We piled our plates with pork chop, beef, heart, kidney, liver, chorizo sausage and cow's udder and tucked in hungrily. It really was delicious. The girls began to lose their reserve and started to chat and enjoy themselves. It was not every day they had an outing to a posh restaurant. The waiter took our photograph and we all gave cheesy grins.

When we had finished eating, I presented each of them with a special Bible. "I am so proud of each one of you young ladies," I began addressing them. "You've all worked super hard to get where you are today. I congratulate you on your achievements and wish you all the very best for the future. You know that if there is ever anything I can do to help you along the way you only have to ask. And now I want to ask you to do a favour for me." The girls looked up from their Bibles puzzled and expectant. "Neither I, nor your sponsors, nor those who have sold the crafts you have made, will ever ask you to repay them. What I would ask you is to pay it forward. All of you have parents and families who have helped you in many ways. Don't ever forget that. Help them, especially in their old age. Some of you have younger siblings. Give them a helping hand as you are able. And in the future, if you are blessed with jobs and earnings and see a neighbour in need, be generous to them also, as God has been generous to you."

In my heart, I acknowledged that in helping these girls, I had discovered God to be kind and generous. In confronting their poverty, and in giving them a helping hand, I had found God to be the One who supplied all our needs and showered us with compassion. I prayed that as they faced the challenges and triumphs to come, they too would discover God to be their All-Sufficient-One.

CHAPTER 19

MOTHERHOOD ON THE FRONT-LINE

It was Monday. I started the morning by giving thanks for another day of life, and the blessings my two little girls brought me. We sat down to eat our breakfast hurriedly, before jumping in the car to drop Tamara off at school. I made it to the health centre just on time.

Señora Maria was first in the door, accompanied by Jacqueline.

"Doctor, I've brought this girl along because I don't know what's wrong with her. Jacqueline has been vomiting for three months now. She can't keep anything down. She's pale and anaemic looking and keeps falling asleep at school. The teacher told me to take her to the doctor."

I sent Jacqueline off to produce a urine sample and then examined her. I only had to lay a hand on her stomach to discover she was pregnant. I called Señora Maria in from behind the curtain.

"Jacqueline is expecting a baby," I told them. Jacqueline burst into tears and Señora Maria started to wail. The ever kind Hortencia came to the rescue.

"Now, now, don't take on so. It's done now," she tried to calm everyone down. "We have to look to the future. Jacqueline, tell us who the father is."

"It is Señor Martin from church," Jacqueline's sister Aracely chipped in, seeing Jacqueline was unable to speak.

"Does he want to live with you?" Hortencia asked.

"No, he's already married. He has a wife and two daughters," Aracely informed us.

"Then you must report him to the authorities, so that he will pay you maintenance for this baby," Hortencia urged them. "How else are you going to support this baby? You need to think of what's best for your child now."

The family went on their way with the medicines they needed, and instructions to return again the following week. Jacqueline's pregnancy was soon public knowledge. She did go to report the father, but he bolted. The police would only go after an errant father if the person reporting him could take the police to him. As Jacqueline did not know where he was, nothing was done.

My father-in-law was angry. "That man has been visiting Jacqueline for a few months, giving the family food. Now we know why. And now that he has her in trouble, he scarpers. It's not the first time he has done this either. He was forced to marry his wife by her family, when he got her pregnant aged fifteen. I heard he did this to another young girl as well. The authorities do nothing. Jacqueline has to find the means to support this child."

"She's still only just starting secondary school, as she missed out on so much schooling when she was younger," I was very disappointed. "I hope the school will be supportive, and that we can help her to achieve at least the basic school certificate."

We were expecting a visitor. Mathieu was a Canadian post-graduate student, coming to do his thesis with us. We had arranged for him to stay with Vladimir's Aunt Estella, and I had a health-needs survey lined up for him to do. We wanted to extend our work into two more villages. Mathieu's task was to find out the needs of the people, so that we could find children needing help and families needing toilets and houses built. We were looking forward to meeting him.

On the day he was due to arrive on the bus in Santo Domingo, Vladimir and I were in town choosing tiles to go in the toilet block on the campsite. Vladimir took the phone call.

"Hello, I'm Mathieu," the voice said.

"Mathieu who?" Vladimir answered, so absorbed in the mesmerising choice of tiles that he had completely forgotten our expected guest. Mortified, I grabbed the phone.

"Hello Mathieu, how nice to hear from you. Are you at the bus station now?" I took over the conversation. "Okay, we're on our way to pick you up."

"How could you forget he was coming?" I gave Vladimir a friendly punch. "What's he going to think of us?"

Mathieu turned out to be a breath of fresh air. He was filled with enthusiasm, ready for anything and more besides. His first language was French, so his Spanish was dotted with many delightful "Oo la las". He fitted into Estella's family like a long lost son and was soon helping her to make her banana fritters at the weekend. He got on with Hortencia and Monserrat like a house on fire.

These lovely ladies accompanied him while he did the survey. They walked for miles, going from house to house in the villages explaining who he was and what he was doing. They braved fierce guard dogs, took no notice of the blazing sun and flapped off intrepid mosquitoes. They calmed those who thought he was a thief, and translated his broken Spanish into more intelligible phrases when necessary. Mathieu thought they were wonderful.

Mathieu, in turn, took them for a trip out to the funfair in town. He made them go on the Ferris wheel, and nearly made them sick with the swinging, twirling, whizzing rides. They talked about that adventure for months to come.

When the time came for him to leave, Mathieu gave Hortencia and Monserrat a T-shirt each. Each T-shirt bore the inscription, "The best nurse in the world." I thought Mathieu had hit the nail on the head with that gift. Both women were extraordinary. They helped me no end, with great skill, despite their lack of education and opportunities in life.

"How old are you?" I asked Hortencia out of curiosity one day, when we were taking our tea break in the health centre.

"Forty-seven," she replied.

"You must've been young when you had your children," I commented, knowing she already had a four-year-old granddaughter.

"I was fifteen when I married," she smiled. "I was very young. We lived in the village up the mountain and hardly ever went to town. I went to primary school and then, when I had finished, my parents were happy to see me married off. They still had eleven other children to look after. I soon had three children of my own. I remember I didn't have much breast milk, so I used to water down cow's milk to feed them. You wouldn't do that nowadays. Life was very simple then. None of the children I was at school with went to secondary school. Life has changed very quickly. My oldest two now have university degrees, and my youngest, despite having her baby aged seventeen is now studying to be a preschool teacher. I'm glad that we have been able to give them opportunities we never had, and that they are doing so well."

"You are a remarkable person," I told her. "You have had great vision for your children. You must have had to sacrifice greatly to get them where they are today."

"Yes, it has been a struggle," Hortencia admitted. "I sent my eldest daughter to stay with my sister in town, so that she could go to secondary school. Then, we moved house so that the younger ones could go. We weren't able to build a house of our own until just a few years ago. Now that my eldest daughter is working, she has helped us to build our house. You have to put their needs first. They are the future. Any mother would do the same."

"You really have created opportunities for them," I congratulated her. "And you are a very close family."

"Oh yes. Even now, my children come and visit me every weekend. I spend the whole of Saturday and Sunday cooking and serving, but I don't mind. It's good to be together, and to go to the mass together. I was very upset when I discovered my youngest was pregnant so very young. I wanted her to finish her studies before having a family. But God is good and it all turned out well in the end. You just have to support your children regardless and help them no matter what. I now have a beautiful granddaughter, who is such a joy to us all. I miss her now my daughter has gone to live in town with her partner. It's good they are finally together as a family, but our little Camilla spent her first four years living in our house."

"She's been like another daughter to you. You must miss her very much. I hope I can be as good a mother as you are," I told Hortencia, who blushed at the compliment.

I found I had to teach Tamara more and more myself at home, so that she was learning what her peers were learning in Britain. She was going to school in the morning and then I was giving her an English lesson in the afternoon, followed by a little maths. She did not have much time left to simply play, before it was time for tea, and bath, and bed.

Soon, I found there was science I wished to show her too, but I was struggling to find the time. I wanted to take her on nature walks through the farm, show her how water could boil and freeze, set up experiments with plants, and so much more. I was concerned that at school everything was done by rote-learning. Nothing was hands on. They were not let loose to investigate for themselves.

"Why am I sending Tamara to school? I still have to teach her everything myself," I asked Vladimir one evening.

"She is learning at school," Vladimir told me. "Today she recited the names of her senses. Did you teach her that in Spanish?"

"No, but I let her investigate what her senses do,"
I informed him. "I blindfolded the girls and got them
to taste things and tell me what they were. Then, they
listened to different sounds and identified them. Then,
we felt things in a bag and tried to work out what they
were. I want them to understand what they are taught,
not just recite lists."

"She has lots of friends at school. Children need to be
with other children and learn to socialise. I don't want
them growing up all shy and timid," Vladimir asserted.

"There is some truth in that, but I think school is
primarily for education, not socialising. There are plenty
of other ways to learn to relate to people, and not just
with children your own age." I replied, letting the
subject drop for then, but resolving to revisit it. I was
beginning to think something was going to have to
change, but I was at a loss to know what to do.

Time flew by, and I could not believe it was Emily's
turn to start nursery. My little baby was now a little
girl. She was still only two, but her birthday was just
six weeks after the start of the school year, and there
was only one entry per year. At first, Emily was excited
that she would be going to nursery. She wanted her
"unicorn" (by which she meant uniform) and new
shoes, and seemed to be looking forward to it.

I duly registered her, and bought her uniform, books
and equipment. Two days before school was due to
start, I received a phone call from the school asking
me to pop in. The Director informed me that they had
just received a memorandum from the Department of
Education telling them the law had changed. Before,
children could start nursery aged two years six months.

Now they had to have had their third birthday by the start of the school year. Emily was still two years ten months, so could no longer register. She would have to wait another year.

"How can the government do this, two days before term starts?" I raged to Vladimir, feeling impotent. "I've bought everything for her already. More to the point, I do not want Emily to be doing the things Tamara is doing at school aged five, when she is six. The discrepancy with Britain will be too big. I will have her reading well at home, and she will only be learning the vowels at school. That is ridiculous."

"What did the Director say we could do?" Vladimir asked.

"She did say we can send her as an observer, but she won't be registered. She will have to repeat the year again next year."

"Maybe we should do that. You never know, the government might change the law again next year so she can progress to the four-year-olds class," Vladimir suggested.

In the end, I did not see what else we could do, so we decided to send her regardless. Tamara now had to be at school at seven-fifteen in the morning. That meant leaving the house at a quarter to seven. Emily was a late riser, despite always being asleep by seven in the evening, so I had to take breakfast with us to give to her in the car outside the school, before she entered at eight o'clock.

When the first day came, Emily did not want to go to nursery. She screamed and clung and wailed. I was taken aback. I hated seeing her like that, but I hardened my heart and left quickly, hoping she would be fine once I had gone. She spent the first morning in Tamara's class.

I tried breaking her in gently, taking her alternate days for a short time only. She continued to wail and scream and refused to go into her classroom. She spent the next few mornings in with her four-year-old cousin, who was also at the school. The teacher told me she cried on and off all morning, not just when I left her. I felt awful. People told me it was normal and to persevere and that she would get used to it. I tried everything: reading her stories about nursery, playing nursery with her dolls, taking her gifts when I picked her up. Nothing worked. I hated seeing my child so upset. It was a relief when she caught a cold and I had the excuse not to take her any more. Once she was better, I tried one more time. She begged me not to leave her. I took her home again.

"I can't do it anymore," I announced to Vladimir that evening. "This has been the worst month of my life. I feel like I am torturing my daughter. If she doesn't want to go to nursery, she's not going to go. She can be with me and her grandmother like before. I can do the activities that she would be doing at nursery with her at home, and she can play with her neighbourhood playmates."

"Well, she's not even registered this year. She's just little. I think it's the best thing to do. Every child is different I guess," Vladimir did not seem to think it was a big deal.

What to do with Tamara, on the other hand, was more of a problem.

CHAPTER 20

PREPARING MY CHILDREN TO LIVE IN A WORLD OF SUFFERING

The disastrous month of trying to take Emily to nursery had so completely absorbed my attention, and my energy, that I had not had the mental strength to think about much else. Now Emily and I were happy again, accompanying each other most of the time and learning to count and to identify colours and shapes in everyday moments, while shopping, reading stories, or pottering on the farm. I felt I was back on track, protecting and moulding my daughter as we faced the bad and the good together. At peace, I opened my eyes to those around me once again.

Jacqueline came for a check-up. She was well, keeping healthy in the pregnancy and continuing to attend school.

"What are your thoughts about school once you have had the baby?" I asked her.

"I talked to the teachers about it and they say I can go to school and take the baby with me while I am breastfeeding," Jacqueline told me. "They're keen for me to continue until I get my basic certificate. That means this year and next year at school."

"I'll talk to your sponsor and see what they think," I promised her. "I hope they'll be willing to continue to support you so that you can finish."

"I wrote a letter to my sponsor," Jacqueline handed me an envelope. "Please can you send it to her? My sisters and brother wrote letters to their sponsors too."

"Yes of course," I replied. "It will be a pleasure."

When Jacqueline had gone, I opened the letters to translate them for the sponsors. Jacqueline had written;

Dear Sponsor,

May God bless you and your family and grant you good health. I am very grateful for your help. I have been studying hard and doing my best at school. I have some news. I am expecting a baby. I am sorry this has happened while I am studying. I love my baby very much but it is difficult to manage. I would like to continue to go to school next year. Will you still support me?

My father has abandoned us and things are hard. My mother does not have work. We are asking God to help us.

Thank you dear Sponsor. May God repay you. May God bless you and your family.

With much affection,
Jacqueline

Her younger brother's letter was written from the heart of a small boy.

Dear Sponsor,
My father has gone. I do not have any toys. Please
can you send me a bicycle?
Love from John.

I had to smile, although I wondered whether to actually send it to the sponsor. I usually instructed the children to write letters of thanks, not begging letters.

I was still chuckling, when Don Dueñas came in walking briskly. "I'm almost completely healed," he pronounced. "I can't wait to go to the hospital and show them my photos. They are barbarians for wanting to cut off my foot."

"Well, they were just doing what they thought was best," I mitigated, looking happily at his foot. The skin was forming over the wound now. It was about half the size it had been.

"Tell him to take his medicine and to watch what he eats," his wife implored. "He thinks he can eat what he wants."

"You must be careful, Don Dueñas," I agreed. "If you don't look after yourself, you will get another foot infection and we might not be able to save it next time."

"No eating sugar or fried foods," Hortencia admonished, looking up from her work on his foot. "If you don't look after yourself, no one else can help you."

"Hmmph," Don Dueñas snorted, "I do try, but a little fried pork is very tempting sometimes."

Hortencia shook her head as he walked out, "There's no telling some people. He's a character that one."

Tania came in with her little baby boy. He was very tiny and cute. She looked enormously happy. We checked him over, and weighed and measured him, and asked how the feeding was going. He just had a little nappy rash, so we gave her some cream.

"My mum is happier now she has this little man to cuddle and take care of," Tania confided. "She has been sad and lonely since Papi died."

"He certainly is a blessing this little one," Hortencia agreed. "He will help your mum enjoy life and look to the future. It's very hard to lose your loved one."

"Yes, she's doing very well. We make sure she's not left alone. We like to keep her company and she sure loves this tiny boy." Tania went on her way content.

At the end of the morning, Hortencia came into the consulting room and shut the door.

"Would you mind having a look at me?" she asked tentatively. "I felt a lump in my breast the other day and it seems to be getting bigger. What do you think it is?"

I looked at her in alarm, and then shook myself. She was young. She was healthy. The chances of this being anything sinister were remote. I felt the lump and was not so sure. The large, craggy mass spoke to my fingers of treachery and betrayal. My heart sank as I imagined the spreading tentacles of disease under her skin.

"It might just be a cyst," I reassured her. "But you should have it checked out. You had a mammogram done not long ago, didn't you?"

"Yes, not more than a year ago, and it was normal."

"You need to go and see the specialist, so they can do an ultrasound and a biopsy to know for certain what this is. Go as soon as you can, so you're not left worrying about it."

I paid national insurance contributions for Hortencia, so I knew she could go to the Insurance Hospital.

I hoped they would give her an appointment quickly. I, for one, could not sleep that night.

I continued to be concerned about what Tamara was doing at school. The teacher sent her homework every day. One day, they were asked to cut out and stick on parts of the body. Tamara cut out arms and feet, a body and a head, a nose and eyes and took her book to her teacher, who marked her down because she was only supposed to put in the parts the teacher had taught her. Tamara had put in extras.

"They should give extra marks for independent thinking, not mark her down," I complained to Vladimir.

"She has to remember what the teacher has taught her," Vladimir explained.

"But that is just rote learning," I argued.

I found most marks were awarded for presentation, not for content, and that they did not have the resources to do experiments or hands on activities. One afternoon, Tamara did not want to colour the picture she had been sent as homework.

"The teacher says I'm the worst at colouring," Tamara huffed, not wanting to try. I was shocked. Tamara had always loved colouring. I never minded if it was not perfectly in the lines. I figured that would come with time. I was upset she had been made to feel bad about doing something she normally enjoyed. It was the last straw. I could not continue sacrificing my daughter's education on the altar of service. There had to be a way of adequately preparing my little one for the world she was living in, or we were going to have to change location.

I started investigating home-education on the internet. I found abundant resources for teaching the British

National Curriculum and much more. There were worksheets, games, videos, unit-studies and lap-books – and many of them were free. I found programmes for studying International GCSEs and virtual sixth form colleges. I found university programmes available online and by distance-learning. The scope for studying at home was abundant and expanding all the time. I could see that the materials I needed to be able to teach the girls for many years to come were freely and readily available.

I also found very supportive Facebook groups, and discovered I agreed with many of their reasons for choosing to home-educate their children. I could see many benefits. The child could study at their own pace and with one-to-one attention. The child would have immediate feedback on their work. The child could investigate their own interests and questions. I loved this idea, as I could see that this would lead to a life-long love of learning. I would have my own children with me, their mother, most of the time still. I would be the person teaching, guiding and influencing them. They would be spending their time with their own family. I could make sure no one bullied them. I would know what they were learning, and be the one to answer their countless questions each day. I could prepare them for an uncertain future and the reality of evil. It would make our lives more flexible. I would no longer have to leave the house before seven o'clock in the morning. Emily could wake and eat at her own pace. They would have time to play.

I lay on my bed in the silence and thought about what it was I wanted my girls to learn. I wanted them to learn to function in both Ecuadorian and British societies. I wanted them to be able to get jobs in either country. They needed to know both Spanish and English well.

I wanted them to learn where to find information, how to investigate the answers to their questions and how to evaluate evidence they were presented with. Growing up with the internet at their fingertips, memorising information was no longer all important. Knowing how to find information, and appraise it, was. I wanted to create in them an endless thirst for knowledge, an interest in the world around them, its peoples and its creatures. I wanted them to learn to be kind, generous women, who would look after the planet and would look out for those around them. I wanted to teach them about the God I love, and whom I believed loved them more than anyone else. I wanted them to grow up secure in the knowledge they are loved, and knowing God's promise to be with us, no matter what tragedies and challenges face us in life.

I was becoming more and more convinced that home-education was the best way forward, but I faced two obstacles. Firstly, I did not see how I could combine it with the work I did for Project Ecuador. Secondly, Vladimir was adamant children needed to go to school.

CHAPTER 21

WHEN GOD SPEAKS

I asked Hortencia how she was getting on arranging an appointment to see the specialist.

"I have to see the general doctor first. They were going to give me an appointment in a month, but as my son-in-law knows the doctor he has agreed to fit me in sooner. I have an appointment next week. He will then refer me to the specialist."

"A month would have been a long time to wait in the circumstances," I agreed. "Let me know how you get on."

I spent spare moments in the health centre thinking about my other problem. I was determined there must be a way to be able to home-educate Tamara, and to continue the work of the charity. I doodled on scraps of paper, trying out different ways of organising my time. Eventually, I came up with a plan. If I taught the girls in the morning at home, and switched working in the health centre to the afternoons, I should be able to fit everything in. I would be able to ask the sewing group and the sponsored children to come and see me in the health centre, instead of at home as they were used to doing. That left trips to schools to promote health and check children for spectacles. Some of that could be delegated to the now experienced Hortencia and Monserrat, and I could do some myself when my girls were on breaks. Paying the monthly bills, which used to require visits to multiple banks had recently been simplified to just two, so should be manageable on a Saturday. My time would be fully occupied, but it was possible.

I had convinced myself it was what I wanted to do, and had decided it would be practical to do so. Now, I just had to convince Vladimir.

"Vladimir, I think it would be much better to take Tamara out of school and for me to teach her at home," I began, confidently. "That way she will be able to learn both languages and cultures, and to a higher standard than she will be able to in a school here in Santo Domingo."

"Children should go to school. Tamara will become shy and timid if she doesn't mix with other children. Besides, you're not a teacher," Vladimir countered.

"I'm quite capable of teaching her, and I know plenty of primary school teachers who will give me help whenever I ask." I was ready for that one. "The internet is full of the resources I need to teach her."

"She needs to be with other children. All children go to school."

"She will have more opportunities to socialise not being in school, than she does at the moment. Teaching her one-to-one, she will need less time in the books and will have lots more time to play. While I am working, she will play with the neighbours. Living, as we do, in the midst of your extended family, the girls have interaction with adults and children every day. Going out and about with me they've already learnt to speak to anyone, and they're not shy. Learning to socialise with a group of other five-year-olds doesn't reflect real life."

"What if you don't want to keep doing it? What if we want to put the girls back into school? What will happen then if they don't have official registration or school reports?" Vladimir was worried.

"Well, if we ever go back to Britain they can just go into the class appropriate to their age. Home-education is recognised and accommodated. I'm not going to put them back into school here. I'm taking this on for the long-term. If it doesn't work, my options are moving to Quito for an International School, for which we would need a lot more money, or going back to Britain."

"You can't know that they're never going to need to go back into the system here. Here, home-education is unheard of. It's not illegal, but it isn't recognised either. You have to be in the system. What will happen if you die and I have to put them back into school? They won't be in the system and they'll be sent back to start school all over again," Vladimir objected.

"Well, it isn't very likely that I will die just yet. What if the education I give them is certified by a teacher in Britain? Then, you could show the authorities they've been studying and put them back into the appropriate school year."

"If you can prove to me I won't have a problem putting them back into school, you can try home-education. If you can't, then they have to go to school," was Vladimir's last word on the matter.

Vladimir went off to visit the Martinez family, who we were planning to build a house for. They had demolished their little room, and were now ready to prepare the ground for the foundations. Their small plot of land sloped steeply at the back, so they needed to fill it in with earth to create a level plot for building on. Vladimir went to give them the instructions on how to build a low wall at the back of the property to retain the earth.

"You will never guess what happened," Señora Martinez was all of a flutter when Vladimir arrived. "My father died a couple of weeks ago. After his death we found out he had sold this plot of land to the neighbour for two hundred dollars. He did it without telling anyone because he had a debt to repay. I only just found out. Now we have the opportunity to build our own house at last, and we have to buy the plot of land back again! The neighbour says he's done a little work to it, so he wants three hundred dollars. I have to use the money we had saved to build the wall at the back to buy the plot back again."

"What a thing to happen!" Vladimir exclaimed. "At least the neighbour will sell it back to you. You could've ended up with no land at all!"

"Yes, I'm very relieved about that," Señora Martinez remarked. "We'll have to save up again to be able to build the wall."

"Perhaps, someone in your family can help you?" Vladimir suggested. "The main thing is to get the wall built. The men who are digging to widen the main road will gladly give you truckloads of earth if you ask them. They need places to dump all the earth they are moving."

"Yes, that's a good idea," Señora Martinez agreed. "That will be a big saving. I'll speak to my brother and see if he could loan us some money for the blocks."

"Let me know when you have done it," Vladimir instructed her. "The couple who have raised money for this house are coming to help build it in a couple of months. It will need to be ready by then."

"We'll let you know for sure, and thank you so much for giving us this opportunity," Señora Martinez was very excited.

Hortencia had her appointment with the general doctor at the Insurance Outpatient Hospital. "The doctor sent me to do another ultrasound and says that it looks benign, but that I should have it removed. He's going to arrange for me to see the specialist, but it will be in about four weeks. He says the specialist will put a needle into the lump to see what it is."

"That's good. It's best to have that test done so you know what it is. Then any operation can be properly planned," I told her.

"The doctor said his father is a breast specialist. He comes to Santo Domingo every Saturday for a private clinic. My daughters said they'll take me this Saturday to see what he says. They're worried that waiting for the other doctor is going to take too long."

"Well, there's no harm in another opinion. You must take into account the cost, mind you. These things can become very expensive."

"Yes, I'm worried about that too. At least the operation is free at the Insurance Hospital. My daughters want to see what the other doctor thinks."

I was puzzling over how best to solve the problem of having home-education recognised as valid by the authorities. I was exploring the idea of a British teacher validating my teaching, but I was not sure it would be accepted by the Ecuadorian authorities, if that eventuality ever arose.

That Saturday, we were just finishing lunch at home on the farm, when some visitors arrived. We went to the open door, wondering who the two cars belonged to. Antonio and Silvana, some friends we had not seen for over a year, piled out of the first car with their daughters, Maria-Victoria and Maria-Gloria.

"Hello," they greeted us. "Your father told us you were here, Vladimir," they explained. "We have visitors this weekend and it's so hot we all fancied a swim. Would it be alright if we swim in your river?"

"Yes, of course," Vladimir responded, as another couple and their two young boys climbed out of the other car. "You're most welcome."

We all put our swimming things on and went down to the river. "How have you been?" Silvana asked me. "It's been too long since we saw you. Time just flies by! Our friends live in Quito. Pedro is from Argentina. He's pastor of a church in Quito. His wife Patty is a psychologist."

"It's lovely to meet you," I smiled.

"Your girls are so big now!" Silvana exclaimed. "The last time we saw you, Emily was just a baby. Where do you have them in school?"

"Tamara has been going to a school in town, but I really want to take her out and teach her at home," I admitted.

"I teach our boys at home," Silvana's friend Patty interjected. I looked at her in surprise.

"I've not met any Ecuadorians who home-school their children," I remarked. "Are your sons registered anywhere?"

"Some Americans suggested it to us, because we had problems with our oldest when he was in nursery. We now have him registered in a school nearby, and he does tests there, but we teach him at home. There's a group of thirty of us who do the same in our part of Quito."

"Wow, that's so interesting," I replied, realising I had just been given the information I needed. "I could do the same with Tamara and that would solve the problem of her not being registered, should she need to re-enter school here later on. I think God sent you here today!"

As we sat chatting and watching the children swim, I marvelled at this answer to prayer. God had sent the person I needed to talk to, right to my door. Now the door was open for me to start our home-education.

I felt very humbled that God would give me the answer I was seeking in this direct way. It was, to me, an expression of His infinite grace. There were so many things I did not understand, so many questions about life and death and suffering that remained unanswered. Yet this touch of kindness encouraged me to continue to trust regardless. It was the undeserved, caress of my loving, Heavenly Father, who was interested in me and cared for me and my family. It was His nudge, telling me to stay put for the time being.

Later that evening, we went to Antonio and Silvana's home for a barbeque. The Argentinean Pastor grilled some delicious Argentinean chorizo and steaks and then read to us from 2 Kings Chapter 20 in which Hezekiah is sick and prays for healing.

"The prophet Isaiah went to Hezekiah and told him God had heard his prayer. He even made time stand still to prove it to him! We can be assured that God hears our prayers and sees our tears, even if God does not grant our request. The times when we do hear a direct answer from God give us the faith to trust when God appears silent," the Pastor taught us, his words striking chords in my heart. As we bowed our heads in prayer together that evening, I acknowledged how little I knew about life and death and the ways of God. So much was clouded in mystery, yet the glimpses I grasped of God were breath-taking. The company of His saints that night was sweet.

Tamara went for her last few days of school. Her class had a trip to the Tsachila Indians planned for the following Friday. It made a special last day for her. She came back excited that she had been able to buy an ice-cream. She said good-bye to her little friends and I gathered all her belongings. We were excited to be moving on.

I went to the local village school. It was one of the schools I helped with sponsors for the children, Christmas gifts and toiletries. They knew me well.

"I want to teach Tamara at home in English, so that she is at the same level as her peers in England," I explained.

"You need to have her registered in a school here or she won't be able to re-enter schooling should she ever want to," the Head-teacher immediately said.

"A friend told me that she has her child registered in a school, but she teaches him at home. Would it be possible to do that with Tamara?" I asked.

"Yes, of course," was the instant response. "I think she should come and do the end-of-term tests, so that we have evidence to show inspectors should there ever be any question of her not attending classes. That would be all."

So I did the necessary paperwork to transfer Tamara to the village school, and we started our home-education adventure.

I told Hortencia and Monserrat about the change, and asked if they could work afternoons instead of mornings. They had no problem with that. We told the regular patients and put up a notice with the new timetable.

"How did you get on with the private doctor?" I asked Hortencia.

"He said he thinks it's benign and no further tests are necessary. He wants to operate and remove the lump next week. He will charge three hundred dollars. The waiting room was full of women he has operated on. He said he is used to feeling these lumps and can tell what they are just by touch. My daughter says she will pay for the operation, but I wonder if it would be better to have it done for free in the Insurance Hospital."

"I would strongly advise you to have the needle test done first," I said. "If he removes it and it turns out to be something nasty, you might well need a second operation."

"It's only two weeks now, until I see the specialist in the Insurance Hospital, so I think I will see what he says," Hortencia agreed. I was relieved that she was going to have the test done.

The first thing I did with Tamara was give her a holiday for a week. Ecuadorian schools had one five-month-long term, two weeks holidays and then another four-months-long term. I thought shorter terms with short breaks in between were a better idea. Besides, I needed time to prepare some classes. I spent every spare moment at Mary's house (where they had the internet) downloading ideas, worksheets and activities to complement what I had already been doing. I planned the first six weeks, after which we would have another short break.

Suddenly, I felt bereft. I had been feeling so positive, that I was caught by surprise by the emotion. I felt scared and unsettled. It was such a radical change in our lives. It was an awesome responsibility. Rather than handing my girls over to professional teachers every day, I was now it, for the foreseeable future. I felt strangely sad that they would be missing out on the "normal" school experience. I worried maybe the girls would get fed up of me teaching them and not cooperate. I feared the unknown, the yet untested waters, and wondered if it would indeed prove to be a success. There was a doubt in the back of my mind that said I had let them down in some way. I knew I was going to have to prove myself to Vladimir, who despite now agreeing to the experiment, was still firmly of the opinion they would be losing something important by not attending school.

But, then I came back to the reasons why I had made this decision, and remembered the perfect timing of Patty's visit, telling me how to go about home-education in Ecuador. We were still there, fighting alongside our friends and neighbours for good. It was time to go forward confidently, trusting in God for His wisdom and provision.

CHAPTER 22

LIVING WITH UNCERTAINTY

The patients adapted to the change in the timetable at the health centre quickly. Don Dueñas came walking in briskly, more to show me his healed foot than to have it dressed. He was very proud of it. It certainly was a most remarkable recovery, and his propaganda had created some unrealistic expectations in other patients.

The next patient came in and asked me to treat his diabetes. I duly asked him what he was taking, and sent him to do some blood tests to see how well it was controlled.

"Come back when you have the test results and I will see if you need a change in your medication or not," I told him.

"But doctor, I was told you would give me medicine to cure my diabetes. You are going to cure me aren't you?"

"There is unfortunately no cure for diabetes. We can cure diabetic ulcers sometimes, but not the disease itself."

"You can't cure diabetes?" the man repeated astounded.

"No, but I can give you medicine to control it," I assured him.

"I already have a doctor who can do that!" he exclaimed, very disgruntled. "I came here so that you could cure me. So, I have come in vain." He picked up his bag and left the room in disgust. I exchanged a look with Hortencia.

"I guess Don Dueñas told him I could cure diabetes. I hope he's not telling many people that!" I commented.

Jacqueline arrived with her baby girl, Emily. She was very tiny and ever so cute. She had tight black curls and light brown skin. Jacqueline was concerned that she had nappy rash and the snuffles.

"And how are you Jacqueline?" I asked.

"I'm doing well. She's such a beautiful baby. I've just returned to school and they're letting me take the baby with me while I am breastfeeding. Some days, my Mum comes with me as well, to look after Emily while I have classes."

"She's putting on weight fine. She must be feeding well. Has the father come back?"

"He said he's going to give me fifty dollars a month. He gave me the first amount this week. He's back living with his wife in Santo Domingo."

"Make sure he does give you the money every month Jacqui, or you should report him again."

Jacqueline nodded. "I have my sewing done. What do you think?"

"It's good." I looked at the hair slides she had made, carefully. "Here's your payment, and please make another twenty for next time."

"Thanks for this work. It really helps." Jacqueline went on her way, baby Emily in her arms.

The next person to see me was Maria-Elena. She was a poor lady whose son was sponsored so that he could attend secondary school, and for whom we had built a house the year before.

"Doctor, I came to bring you Juan's latest school report," Maria-Elena began. "I also thought I should warn you, some of the bad people in the village keep asking about you. They ask me what you have on the farm, what kind of car you have, and if you have any security in place, that kind of thing. I don't tell them anything, but you should be careful. I think they have their eye on you."

I did not quite know what to make of that information, so I put it to the back of my mind, resolving to mention it to Vladimir later on.

Piedad was the next patient. Her face was even more swollen with tumour and she was thinner.

"Good afternoon, dear Doctor. How are you dear Doctor?" she began. "I've had a lot of bleeding from the tumour and I wonder if you can help me." She stopped to dab at the seeping monstrosity with her handkerchief. "I feel quite weak with all the blood loss."

"Yes, of course," I responded, as Hortencia came forward to clean the tumour. She expertly applied epinephrine to the bleeding points and dressed the open sores. I did a blood test for anaemia and found Piedad was suffering from it, so we gave her some iron syrup to take. The hole in her palate made eating solids and taking tablets difficult for her now.

Piedad was grateful, as ever, for the little help we could give her, and left all smiles and thanks.

Hortencia came in and sat down next, "I saw the specialist at the Insurance hospital and he's going to do the needle test next Tuesday afternoon, so I won't be able to work that day," she said.

"I'm glad he is going to do the test. Don't worry about work: you must look after yourself first. I hope the results are negative and you can be reassured."

"I hope so too. I don't know what I shall do if it's cancer. I've seen so many patients with horrible tumours working here." Hortencia could not go on, as tears filled her eyes.

"I'm sorry," I consoled her. "I wish I could tell you everything is okay right now. You mustn't think you're going to end up like Piedad, or other patients you've seen here. They had very advanced diseases and didn't have proper treatment. Even if you are told you have cancer, you must know it's very early. There are good treatments available for this now."

"Yes," Hortencia nodded, "it's very hard waiting to find out."

I wished I could speed up the process for this dear, gentle friend, but there was really nothing I could do. All we could do was to keep her company during the wait.

* * *

The first few weeks of home-education felt quite strange. It was great that we no longer had to get up at the crack of dawn. Tamara was an early riser, so she had plenty of time to eat and dress before starting her studies. Emily could sleep in longer, as was her rhythm, and eat while I started teaching Tamara. We took a little while to settle into a routine that suited us, but, with each day that passed, we found ourselves adapting more and more. Emily was jealous of the attention I was giving Tamara, so we included her too in games, songs and activities. I think the strangest thing was having these four hours in a morning to give the girls my undivided attention. I loved it. I wished I had done it sooner.

I discovered they each had different learning styles. Tamara was very active - a kinaesthetic learner. She learnt best while moving around. Skip-counting on hopscotches and counting while jumping on the trampoline worked well for her. Emily was an auditory learner. She learnt her alphabet and numbers best while singing songs. I enjoyed being able to make learning fun for them. As we began to find our feet and relax into our programme, we found we had plenty of time for reading the stories that the girls never tired of. We did stacks of painting, sewing and sticking, creating and acting. We got to know each other better.

I thanked God for each precious moment with my girls. I counted it a real privilege to be able to spend time with them. They were growing up so fast. I knew that in the blink of an eye they would be teenagers. Tamara's idea of a Saturday treat was to listen to me read *The Faraway Tree* aloud and to bake cupcakes. I wanted to cherish them being little and innocent, with unfiltered curiosity and unlimited energy.

I loved being the one to share these wonderful experiences with them. I will never forget the look on Tamara's face, when she took water out of the freezer and found it had turned into ice. She thought it was magic. I would not have missed out on showing them ants' nests and wiggly worms for the world. It was such fun to show them how to do "invisible" pictures with wax candles and black paint. It was hard work, and required preparation, but it was definitely worth it.

One of the lads who cut our bananas came to our house, quite agitated, early one Sunday morning. Vladimir went out to talk to him. When he came back, he looked worried.

"The lad was saying that they were robbed on Thursday evening. The thieves arrived at their house with a lorry and stripped the house bare. The thieves knew the family had just sold some manioc and had the money in the house. The thieves arrived when they were still outside the house, tied them up and beat them. He came to warn us we should be alert, because we are isolated here with no neighbours nearby."

"I forgot to tell you Maria-Elena came to warn me of the same thing the other day," I commented, feeling worried. "Then someone else told me their neighbour was stolen from in broad daylight. The thieves gave a hypnotic drug to the owners of the house, so they helped to load their own possessions on to the thieves' lorry. Can you imagine that? It wasn't until the lorry drove off that the neighbours realised there was something wrong and raised the alarm."

"There have been other robberies recently on isolated farms. They always seem to know when a lorry is coming back from Quito having sold bananas, so they will have cash on them. A man was killed on the road near here a couple of weeks ago, when thieves stole his car. I didn't want to worry you, but maybe we should think about moving until we can make the farm more secure."

"What can we do?" I asked.

"I think we need to build a little house for another family to live here on the farm with us. It's harder for thieves to take two families by surprise at once. I'm going to put an alarm system in. I'll do it with sensors, so it comes on if anyone moves outside near the house at night. You should always be inside the house with the doors locked by six o'clock in the evening. Maybe we should go and stay at Fred and Mary's until I do these things."

"Do you think it's necessary?" I asked, not really wanting to have to move all my things.

"I'm worried. What if something happens to the girls?"

Fred and Mary had just gone on a visit to England, so I contacted them there to ask if we could move to their house temporarily. They, of course, agreed. Vladimir quickly had the alarm installed and we adopted precautions such as being locked inside our house before dark. The workmen started building a little house on the farm within sight of our own. Vladimir also installed an alarm in the neighbour's house at the top of our track, and we listened out for each other being in trouble.

I was shocked to discover that I was reluctant to actually move out. Vladimir continued to try to persuade me.

"My love, I am really worried. I couldn't stand something happening to you or the girls. Why don't we move up the road, just for a little while?"

"But if we go, who will look after the farm and the animals? There are workers on the farm all day long. It's only at night we're alone," I remonstrated.

"What's happened to you?" Vladimir asked. "Usually, you're the first to take every precaution!"

"It's just so hard to quantify the danger we're in," I replied. "I'm not surprised by the threats this time. I just don't want thieves to chase me out of my own home." I paused to reflect for a moment. "I said "home"," I exclaimed, "I do feel at home on the farm. We're making it our own. I don't want to panic or to live in fear. I know there are no guarantees. I just want to live my life in peace, taking a day at a time. Please can we stay at home. You'll soon have the house for care-takers built on the farm. That will make it safer."

"I like this new, brave you!" Vladimir grinned, agreeing to stay put.

I did write an email asking friends to pray about the situation. We remained on high alert, but I felt at peace.

Hortencia had the needle test done and the result was inconclusive. The specialist now recommended an open biopsy. To have this done, Hortencia had to go to Quito. First, she had tests done to make sure she was fit for an anaesthetic. She had a cough and cold, so she had to wait an extra week to get the all-clear for the procedure to be done. Once it was done, she had to wait again for the results. It was now three months since she had told me about the lump. It felt like it was taking a very long time to get to a diagnosis. To poor Hortencia, who was the soul of patience, it must have been an eternity.

The Martinez family had their wall built and plot of land filled in and levelled out. They were ready for the building of their new house to begin. The couple who had raised the funds, Lee and Rachel, were on their way to Ecuador. They were still in the USA, when they heard about my email requesting prayer because of the threat of thieves. Suddenly, I received a worried message.

"It sounds like things are dangerous where you are at the moment. We really want to come and build the house, but we are wondering if it is safe and wise to do so?"

Their message took me by surprise. I was taken aback how much my perception of risk had changed over my time ensconced in Ecuador. A few years back, that would have been me asking the question.

"The thieves are targeting isolated farms like ours," I responded, reassuring them. "You will be staying with Fred and Mary. There are plenty of people about there, as they are in the middle of the village. Nothing will happen at their house." I was sure they would be fine.

Lee and Rachel decided to go ahead with their plans, and we were soon at the airport to pick them up.

They came out into the arrivals hall all smiles and full of enthusiasm. They were a bright young couple, who seemed to radiate happiness. They immediately made us laugh, and it felt like we had known them for ages. They enjoyed their first Ecuadorian meal with gusto, and then we drove down the mountain telling them all about Santo Domingo, until sleepiness overtook them. They were soon installed in Fred and Mary's house and ready to get started on building the house.

One of the first things they had to get used to was the disorganisation and inefficiency in Ecuador. There was always one thing or another that meant trying to get things done took longer than one planned. They were very patient and went with Vladimir to order and buy the materials needed to start on the house, and after a week or so, they were ready to begin wielding spades.

Señora Martinez was overwhelmed to see her dream becoming a reality. So much was promised in Ecuador, and so little delivered. I had learnt never to believe something was really going to happen, until I saw it in progress with my own eyes. Señora Martinez could now see the foundations of her house being dug, and the smile never left her glowing face.

Lee and Rachel were both hard workers. They put on their old clothes, slapped on the sun-cream and floppy hats, and sieved sand, mixed cement and laid blocks with the best of them. They managed to communicate with the other workmen with their pigeon Spanish and sign language, and were soon picking up useful Spanish phrases. The workmen thought they were wonderful.

Rachel was a teacher, and Lee a social worker. They had come for ten weeks to work voluntarily and paid their own way.

"It's amazing they're willing to give up their time and money to come and help like they are," Vladimir commented one evening, after being on the worksite with them most of the day. "I hope they enjoy their time here. We must show them something of Ecuador too. They can't come to my amazing country and just see Santo Domingo."

"I think they're genuinely glad to have this chance to help people less fortunate than themselves," I responded. "I'm sure they'll be glad they came."

Hortencia had the biopsy done, and waited a fortnight for the results to come through. Her daughter telephoned me.

"My mother has her results and they show cancer. She's taking the results to you, for you to explain them to her. The doctor in the hospital didn't tell her much. He just said that they're going to operate. Please don't upset her. We want her to be calm for the surgery."

Hortencia handed me her results later that day. "I have cancer, don't I?" she asked in a small voice. My heart broke for this precious woman, who would not even hurt a fly. She certainly had done nothing to deserve this calamity in her life. If ever I was tempted to ask why someone had to suffer, it was now.

"Yes, the results show cancer cells," I responded as gently as I could. "What did the doctor say he is going to do?"

"He told me he's going to remove my breast. Then he'll give me chemotherapy."

"When he operates, he'll check that he has removed it all. It's been caught early, so he should be able to. The chemotherapy afterwards is to kill off any cancer cells that might have spread elsewhere in your body, so that the cancer doesn't come back," I explained. Hortencia nodded in understanding.

"I trust in God," she stated quietly. "I can only bow to His will. He will give me the strength I need to face this. My daughters are very worried. My eldest is going to take time off work to come with me to Quito for the operation. She will take good care of me. My youngest daughter is going to look after me, once they send me home again."

I had tears in my eyes, as I listened to this brave, faithful woman. Looking at her, I could trust that God would give her the resources she needed to face this huge crisis in her life. I promised to pray for her as she walked through this valley of the shadow of death. I knew she was not alone. Her Heavenly Father would be with her every step of the way, no matter what the outcome was. She was going to suffer pain, anxiety, vomiting, hair loss, and traumatic surgery. Only God knew why. I hoped I could help a little by being a friend at this time of need.

CHAPTER 23

LIVING WITH GOD'S HELP

Many friends responded to my request for prayer for our security, and we did not hear of any more break-ins for several weeks. The main road at the end of our track was being widened, and our entrance was made impassable for lorries due to the thick mud on the incline. No thieves would be able to drive a lorry in to steal anything significant for a while anyway. The alarm system was working, and the little house we were building on the farm was almost finished. (Work had been suspended temporarily so that the workmen could help Lee and Rachel to build the Martinez house.) We remained vigilant and were careful to be inside before dark. We were thankful nothing untoward seemed to be happening. All we could hear of an evening was the buzz of the insects, and the distant crashes made by the dumper trucks working on the road.

Lee and Rachel were making great progress on the Martinez house. The walls were going up fast and soon the roof could be put on. They were content to see the work going ahead and were enjoying the banter with the locals.

"Don't you mind not being able to go out in the evenings?" Rachel asked me one day. "One of the things Lee and I love to do at home is to go for a walk in the evening. I would really miss that after a while."

"I suppose I've got used to it," I replied. "We don't like to leave the house empty in the evening, so we entertain ourselves at home. There's usually plenty to keep us occupied! How are you getting on at Fred and Mary's?"

"Oh, they're great!" Rachel's response was immediate. "They're such amazing people. Just imagine, Fred is over seventy and still running a farm and giving local people jobs. That's not to mention all he does for the church and the community. He works so hard. Mary is such a kind person, and a first-class hostess. I feel like we're living in luxury and being pampered all the time!"

"They are incredible," I agreed. "Mary's helped me so much with the girls. She's an extra grandmother to them. They are both the souls of generosity to friends and neighbours alike."

Hortencia had her mastectomy, five months after she first noticed the lump. It felt an awfully long time to diagnosis, but at least she was having it dealt with professionally, and only had to pay for journeys to Quito and a few odds and ends, not the surgery itself. When I saw her after the operation, she was sore but optimistic.

"My arm is very painful, but they gave me exercises to do that they say will help make it better," she told me. "The surgeon said he removed it all, and some glands to check it hadn't spread."

"I hope they're clear, so you can be sure it was all removed," I tried to encourage her.

"It's hard not having a breast anymore," Hortencia choked up a little, and looked at me with tears in her eyes. "It doesn't feel right."

"I can't imagine how that feels," I acknowledged. "You could have one reconstructed later on, if you want to."

Hortencia gulped, and nodded, and smiled again through the mist of tears. "I'm grateful for all that's being done for me. I'm to start chemotherapy in three weeks' time. I wonder what that's going to be like. They're going to give me six doses, each one three weeks apart."

"It can be gruelling," I warned her. "You have to remember it's going to do you good and make you well again. Just concentrate on getting through it, so you can recover full health. God will be with you."

Vladimir kept his word and decided to take Lee and Rachel to Otavalo, in the north of Ecuador, for a long weekend. He was determined that they should admire something of his beautiful country. We set off up the mountain road, Lee and Rachel comfortably accommodated in the back of the truck, under a canvas roof, seated on cushions and blankets.

Our first stop was the Middle of the World. This was the equator monument, situated just outside of Quito. We posed on the line to take photographs, and then enjoyed lunch.

"I can't believe I feel cold on the equator!" Rachel laughed. "I have goose bumps, look!"

"We're at ten thousand feet above sea level here. That's why it feels cold," I explained.

The complex had a display of varied insects. The girls loved looking at them.

"This is perfect for our mini-beasts project!" I exclaimed. The girls liked the butterflies that looked like owls best, and I was rather taken with the huge, shiny beetles on display. The range of insects that had been collected was amazing, and I was sure there were many more to be found.

We went on to Otavalo, and found a rustic hostel to stay in. The owners were very friendly. Our balconies looked out over the potato fields and a beautiful lake. We could see the indigenous people in their traditional dress, working the land and driving the cattle. It was a remarkable place to stay.

The next day Tamara was very excited. She remembered our previous visit to the area, two years before.

"Let's go to the volcano crater!" she cried. "They have the most delicious *empanadas* with sugar in the world!" We all smiled at her enthusiasm and memory for all things sweet.

The crater had been made by an eruption, many years before. The volcano was still active. The crater was about three kilometres in diameter and full of water creating a large lake. We went on a little boat ride to see bubbles of gas rising to the surface. As we gazed, astounded, at the immense hole that had been blasted in the mountain, our minds boggled at the force of the eruption. I wondered too at the powerful God, who had created this staggering volcano.

After the boat ride, we sat down for our *empanadas* and Tamara was delighted.

"See how delicious they are," she exclaimed to us all, very pleased we were following her recommendation.

Later that day, Rachel and Lee decided this was their chance to try the famous guinea pig. We went to a good restaurant and ordered them the traditional dish. It was served on a large patter, head and all.

"I don't think it would be so bad, if it weren't that you have to look into its eyes and see its toothy grin," Rachel sighed.

Lee thought it tasted similar to duck, and ate a decent portion. Rachel was not so convinced. Vladimir willingly helped them finish off their dinner, sucking the beast down to the bones. All that remained was the head.

"People here eat the brains as well," Vladimir teased, wondering how adventurous Lee would be.

"That's disgusting," Rachel cried.

"No. I'll give them a try," Lee agreed. Vladimir scooped some jelly-like grey stuff out of the head and handed it to Lee on a spoon with a grin. Lee gulped and put it in his mouth. His expression was hilarious.

"The brains are not the best bit then?" I suggested wryly.

"I think I'll stick to the legs next time," Lee spluttered reaching for his glass of water in a hurry. The rest of us collapsed in giggles.

The next morning, we visited the famous Otavalo market. The main square was filled to the brim with brightly coloured wall hangings, paintings, bags and handicrafts. The air was filled with the traditional panpipe music and the square was bustling with people. The Otavalo people were dressed in their traditional ponchos, shawls and hats adding to the ambience. We wandered through the stalls in delight, taking in all the sights, sounds and smells.

"These shawls are such a bargain," Rachel was in shopping heaven. "I'm going to get some for my sisters."

"Papi, can you buy me this hat?" Emily asked, fingering a white and pink crocheted bonnet longingly.

"Mummy, can I have this little pot to keep my rings in?" Tamara asked, pointing out a small, leather, heart-shaped pot, with matching lid.

"We could be here all day and keep seeing things we would like," I laughed, as we found yet more stalls to enjoy.

However, duty called and we had to start our journey back to Santo Domingo. We arrived back dusty and tired, but satisfied that Lee and Rachel had at least had a glimpse of some of the amazing scenery and colourful peoples that make up the country of Ecuador.

A few days later, we picked up Lee and Rachel, to take them to the building site as usual, only to be shocked by their news.

"You will never guess what happened last night," they began. "We were still up playing cards with Mary, when there was a knock at the door. We were going to open it, but Mary stopped us and made us ask who it was first. The person at the door wouldn't say who they were, so we didn't open the door. A short while later, Fred went out to investigate and found that someone had loosened the light bulbs around the garage, so the lights were all out. The lock on the garage door was broken and many of his expensive tools were lain out on the ground, as if they were ready to be loaded on to the lorry and stolen."

I was stunned. I was mortified. I was concerned for them all. A thousand thoughts filled my head. Why would anyone steal from gentle, generous Fred and

Mary? How come no one had heard anything? I had assured Lee and Rachel that by staying with Fred and Mary they would be safe from thieves. Now what would they think? What if something had happened to them? What if they had opened the door? Rachel took up the tale.

"Fred thinks the person at the door maybe wanted to get the keys to steal the lorry with the tools. I'm so glad we didn't open the door. They might have had a gun. I can't believe we didn't hear them breaking in. I suppose it's the racket the diggers and dumper trucks are making, day and night, right outside the house at the moment, that meant that we didn't hear anything. I suppose the thieves were taking advantage of that."

"Maybe the person at the door came to warn us, but it's strange they didn't want to say their name," Lee suggested.

"I'm very glad you didn't open the door," I breathed. "Imagine if anything had happened to you. How awful it all is. It must be the noise of the diggers they took advantage of, because normally the neighbours would have heard something too."

"I'm going to install an alarm system for Fred," Vladimir asserted. "We can put a couple of sensors in the garage, so that if anyone tries that again, a siren will go off. Everyone will hear that: diggers or no diggers."

"That is an excellent idea," I agreed. "You really don't know what is going to happen next in this life. I'm just so glad no harm came to any of you. God was gracious in protecting you."

CHAPTER 24

WORKING FOR CHANGE

Hortencia came to see me at the health centre a few days after her first round of chemotherapy. She looked pale and very thin.

"The hospital gave me a sick note to have three days off work after the chemotherapy," Hortencia began. "They told me I should put a mask on, and go to work."

I looked at her in horror. She didn't look well enough to be out and about, let alone at work.

"How do you feel?" I asked her, gently.

"I keep being sick. It's starting to wear off. I can't eat anything. My arm is still very painful. I don't have any more pain-killers. I came to ask if you could give me some more."

"You're not to come back to work, until you are well," I told her in no uncertain terms. "You're at risk of infections here, as your defences are lowered by the chemotherapy. You don't look strong enough to work at the moment. You need to rest and recover, ready to face the next round of chemotherapy. Don't worry. I will pay your National Insurance contributions regardless, so that they don't refuse to treat you. Of course, I can give you some more tablets for the pain."

"Thank you," Hortencia breathed. "I really want to return to working here, but I don't feel able to at the moment. Thank you for paying the National Insurance each month. The first thing they do, when I turn up for an appointment, is check that I have paid."

"Don't worry about a thing," I replied. "No one should expect you to work at the moment. Go home and rest."

"I can't believe the hospital expects people undergoing chemotherapy to continue to work." I remarked to Vladimir once I was home again. "Hortencia is going through a gruelling treatment at the moment, and needs all the help and support she can get. She doesn't need to be worrying about working. Each time she has the chemotherapy, she has to go the three hours on the bus to Quito the day before, and have the blood tests done. Then, she has to stay overnight in a hostel, at her own expense, and attend for the chemotherapy the next day. Part of the medicine is out of stock in the Insurance Hospital just now, so they have to go and buy that from a private pharmacy and have it ready. After the chemotherapy, she stays another night in Quito, before facing that dreadful journey home. The hairpin bends are enough to make anyone sick, let alone someone who has just been pumped full of medicine that makes them vomit."

"I hope you told her not to worry about work at the moment," Vladimir commented.

"Of course," I assured him. "I can't believe all this is happening to Hortencia. She's so young to have cancer.

I mean, I know I see young patients with cancer all the time, but it happening to a friend is different somehow. It makes me think it could happen to me too."

"We never know what might be around the corner," Vladimir agreed. "How is Hortencia coping?"

"She is very weak and low at the moment. All she can do is take a day at a time. We must pray the treatment does its job, and that she comes out of all this well again."

Vladimir took my hand, and we lay on our backs on our bed contemplating life.

"Let's give thanks for another day of life," I thought out loud. "Let's celebrate every joy, while we have the chance, and live generously towards those around us. Let's give thanks for two healthy daughters and the time we have with them. Let's enjoy every moment we have to delight in God's creation."

"Come on then," Vladimir laughed, jumping up from the bed with a sudden burst of energy. "Let's look after the farm God has given us. There are chickens to be fed and lemons to be picked."

We ran off towards the chicken house, calling to the girls to follow. Suddenly, Vladimir signalled us all to be quiet. Over our heads flew an eagle. The powerful, graceful bird circled over the fish pool. We all stood transfixed, watching this elegant bird. All at once, he dove straight down into the water and rose up clutching a fish. It all happened in seconds. Then, he was off, flying away over the banana plants into the distance.

"Did you see that?" I cried. "What an amazing bird!"

"I've seen that eagle before, but I don't like to scare it off: it's too beautiful. Let him have a few of the fish," Vladimir smiled.

"Papi, can I feed the fish?" Tamara asked.

"Of course," Vladimir replied, giving her a pot full of fish food to scatter on the water.

"I've collected the eggs," Emily giggled.

"Well done. What else needs doing?" I asked.

"We need to clip the wings of that cockerel which keeps jumping into the chicks' pen," Vladimir replied. "You grab it Andy!"

I was not at all keen on this suggestion, but decided this was not the moment to be squeamish. Bravely, I climbed into the pen, and launched myself at the cockerel that tried to run, but could not escape my clutches.

"I've got him!" I yelled triumphantly, as I held him tight and waited for Vladimir to appear with the scissors. "Hurry up, or he will get away!" I was feeling very proud of myself for being so bold.

The wings cut, and the chicks safe, we set off up the hill on the farm to pick some lemons. These green lemons grew, fat and juicy, on an old tree in the middle of the banana plants. Vladimir and I grabbed sticks to knock them down, while the girls gathered them into a bucket. We soon had plenty to make juice, lemon curd and lemon cakes with.

"I love being more self-sufficient," I exclaimed. "It's such a help to have our own chickens, eggs, fish, lemons, bananas, guanabanas and maize. What a blessing this is."

"I like the baby chicks," Emily chimed in. She loved holding and stroking them.

"I like making lemon juice with sugar in," Tamara added, sucking her fingers.

"It's good to have work to do and fruits of our labours to enjoy," Vladimir contributed.

Señora Maria and sixteen-year-old Aracely came to see me in the health centre. They were both suffering from stomach pains. I gave them medicine for gastritis and parasites, and told them to take one of the medicines three times a day, after meals. I was surprised when they came back to see me a week later not much better.

"Did you take the medicine?" I asked them.

"There's no point in lying is there, Doctor?" Señora Maria began. "We've taken some of the medicine, but you told us we had to take it after meals. We don't always have food to eat three times a day, so we couldn't take the medicine regularly, because we couldn't eat regularly."

My hands itched to give them the food from my cupboards. "Well, that's why you have gastritis," I explained. "You need to eat regularly to be healthy."

"I can't find work," Señora Maria lamented. "I wash clothes for people when they want me to, but it doesn't earn me much, and sometimes no one wants their clothes washed. I don't know how to do anything else."

"Can you give me sewing work as well to help?" Aracely asked.

"I'll see what I can do," I nodded. "The problem is selling enough of the goods you all produce."

"May God replay you for all you do to help us," Señora Maria pronounced.

I looked at Aracely and smiled, "This is why I find sponsors for you all to go to school. It's so important you get an education, so you can find jobs later on. Otherwise, you will end up in the same plight as your mother. Make sure you take advantage of this opportunity, and study hard."

I thought of the times I had complained about getting up on a Monday morning to go to work. I remembered with shame the times I had treated work as a chore: something to be got through so that I could enjoy the weekends and holidays. I realised that work was a blessing and a privilege. People all around me were desperate for work. They worked every day they were offered, and still did not have enough money to feed their large families adequately. I had hardly ever heard of a family in the village going on a holiday. People lived their lives from day to day, until the day they died. To have money to buy food and clothing was a daily fight. Anything else was an unheard of luxury.

I, through no merit of my own, had received a good education, which had equipped me for work in highly paid jobs. I turned to God in thankfulness for the blessing of work, for a meaningful occupation and for many ways of filling my time. I thanked God for the payment I received financially, and also in personal fulfilment. I thanked God I had what I needed, each and every day, and more besides to share with my neighbours.

That afternoon, a patient gave me some fish to thank me for healing his leg ulcer. I took the bag round to Señora Maria's after work, and her son, John, eagerly fell to gutting the fish. I was glad I could share a meal with them.

Lee and Rachel were enjoying donating their hard work, and seeing the Martinez house nearing completion. Vladimir went to do the electrical wiring and Lee helped pull the cables through the pipes in the walls and connect the switches. Rachel assisted laying the tiles on the kitchen bench, brightening up the room with vivid green ceramics. Señora Martinez supplied them with jugs of lemon juice and her two children eagerly tried to help whenever they could. The carpenter came and fixed on the front door, and Lee learnt to solder, while making the window protections from iron rods.

"We won't put the light bulbs, toilet bowl and basin in, until the doors and window protections are on," Señora Martinez explained, when Rachel asked her why they did not get the bathroom ready. "There are many thieves in this part of the village. They would come and steal the toilet if the house isn't secure."

"I'm so glad we're able to provide you with a secure house," Rachel responded. "Now you'll be able to enjoy a safe place to live and be able to look after your things well."

"I can't tell you how wonderful it is for me to have a house with bedrooms, and a water-proof roof for my children to sleep under. What was an impossible dream, has come true," Señora Martinez said, teary-eyed.

Señora Martinez cooked her best chicken for Lee and Rachel, and the other workmen. She served them all with rice and fizzy juice, and told them the story of how she had had to buy her lot of land back from her neighbour, after her father had sold it. She, her husband and their two children, all thanked them profusely for the indescribable gift of a house of their own. It was a time for celebration, a new start in their lives.

"I can't imagine ever going back to normal life after this," Rachel commented to me later. "I don't think either of us has been involved in anything more worthwhile, ever. It's simply incredible, to see a family with a home that they couldn't have had without the support of others. It's so remarkably basic too; a house with solid walls, running water and a flushing toilet. It highlights our responsibility to give of our time and money for those whose needs are imminent. Somehow, when you see it in the flesh, it's a mixture of great and appalling. It's fantastic to see a family receive a house, but it's also an uncomfortable reminder of how luxurious our own lives are. I literally cannot admit to people here that we're travelling in Australia after this. People here don't go travelling! They work, and work, and try to get a house, and hope to have enough food for their families, and hope to pay for medical bills when they come."

"We really hope, in our lives, to use our money and time more thoughtfully, as there are families whose lives could and would be changed forever if we did," Lee agreed. "And really, what on earth could be a better use of money or time?"

"It's been such an incredible experience, to be able to give a family a house, and actually help to build it ourselves," Rachel exclaimed.

"It's wonderful to know we raised enough money to build about three more houses yet," Lee agreed. "We would love to be staying to help build them too. However, the reality is, one can't live as volunteers forever."

"Maybe you'll be back again, one day," I suggested with a cheeky grin. "You would be most welcome anytime."

"We need to celebrate this wonderful achievement," Vladimir said decidedly. "I'm going to take you both out to a nice Italian restaurant I know in town, this evening. The gift of a house for a family can't go unmarked."

That evening, we left the girls with their grandparents, and had a rare evening out in town. As we called to pick up Lee and Rachel, they hesitated to answer the door, still wary of thieves. Once we convinced them it was only us, we were soon on our way into town. We all relaxed. The restaurant was a small cosy place that Vladimir and I had been to a handful of times before, on special occasions. The food was mouth-wateringly delicious. It was a real treat. As the boys debated which seafood dish to try, we laughed, and joked, and told anecdotes. Lee and Rachel had been a real pleasure to have around. We were going to miss them, when they headed on their way.

"This is a toast to finishing a house for the Martinez family," Vladimir proposed. As we chinked our glasses, he continued, "This is the fifth house we have built through Project Ecuador, and we still have funds for more. This is a great achievement."

We celebrated in style, and enjoyed our evening very much. I thought Rachel's earlier comment was very true. I would find it hard to return to "normal" life in Britain. I could certainly never ignore the plight of my friends in this corner of the world, nor forget their suffering. Living beside them had changed me, and continued to do so. I thanked God for the chance to help them in a practical way, every day.

CHAPTER 25

FIGHTING THE GOOD FIGHT

Doña Elvira mourned the loss of her son, Emilio, for many months, but never asked God why He had allowed this terrible tragedy to happen to her son. She was humble before her God. She knew that accidents happen, each and every day. She did not consider herself better than anyone else. She did not think she should be immune to this world's suffering. She cried out to God for His help to bear the heart-breaking pain, and for a way to live into the future.

A short time after Emilio's death, Doña Elvira's daughter fell pregnant. Doña Elvira began to take an interest in life again, as she started to cook nourishing soups for her daughter and the tiny baby growing in her womb. As the baby grew, Doña Elvira became increasingly concerned for her daughter and her unborn grandchild. Gradually, almost imperceptibly, she began to live life again. When baby Lucas was born, Doña Elvira threw herself into helping her daughter care for him. This new, precious life to love and care for, gave her new purpose and consolation. She found a reason to live again.

If living in Ecuador has taught me one thing, it is that life is unpredictable. You never know what might happen next. Witnessing the daily traumas that happen to the people around me has sparked in me a new humility. I have realised that our world is fallen and imperfect. There is no rhyme or reason why tragedy strikes, most of the time. There is no reason why this world's sadness may not affect me too.

Piedad continues to live with her disfiguring facial tumour. Every day, she clutches her cloth to dab away the liquid that constantly drips from her wound. Every day, she bears the constant pain. Yet, every day, she enjoys the company of her grandchildren and receives the ministrations of her daughters. She has taught me that life is but a breath. Every day, no matter how imperfect, is a gift. She shows me that life itself has great value, and is worth fighting for. She has shown me that when help is needed, God is close.

Hortencia is now undergoing her second phase of chemotherapy. She is putting on weight and feeling much better than she did. She puts me to shame with her courage and faith. She unswervingly trusts in her Heavenly Father to give her the strength she needs each day, to face whatever it throws at her. When I see her, she asks about me and the girls and wants to know that we are all well. She is more concerned about others, than herself.

The other Saturday, Tamara and Emily went to play with Hortencia's grand-daughter at Hortencia's house. I arrived to find the girls sliding down a pile of sand - filthy, but having the time of their lives. As I sat and chatted to Hortencia, she was full of news about her family and laughing at the girls with their rough and tumble.

"It does me good to see them playing outside, as takes their fancy," Hortencia chuckled. "Camilla lives in town now and spends the afternoons in an apartment. She loves coming to visit me in the countryside and having the freedom to play. She has really enjoyed having your girls to play with this afternoon."

"My girls have loved it too. I don't know how I'm going to convince them it's time to go home for a shower!" I exclaimed.

Hortencia has taught me not to be afraid of the future. Fear just serves to sap my energy and fill me with paralysing anxiety. It does not change anything. We can take reasonable precautions against known dangers and threats, and try to prevent accidents, but we can never know what will happen tomorrow or escape all of life's tragedies. We can place our hope in God, no matter what tomorrow brings. As I seek to live this life that God has granted me and called me to, I try to make the most of every opportunity. I want to celebrate the joys with enthusiasm. I want to try something new when I have the chance. I want to share His love as He has loved me so much. I want to face the challenges of life with courage. I want to endure the sorrows, trusting in Him for comfort and hope.

The last time Lorena came to bring me her sewing, she was, as ever, unfailingly polite and respectful. She smiled her celestial smile, as she showed me the colourful Andean pencil cases she had made, and told me of the dance she was to participate in at school. If you did not know of the death of her father, you would never have guessed from her brave attitude to life. I am full of admiration for the resolute way in which she is pursuing her studies and supporting her mother. She is abidingly grateful for the help of her sponsor and the income from the sewing project. Behind the smile there is, of course, sorrow for the father she has lost, but Lorena has allowed this pain to mould her into a sensitive friend. There is no trace of bitterness to be found in her beautiful countenance. She is quick to spot a soul in need and to reach out a helping hand. It is a privilege to be able to help her. I can only pray that, in the knocks and trials of life, I will be as malleable.

When I think of the dire plight of women such as Señora Maria, Esther and Jacqueline, trying to raise their children without a living wage, and indeed the worse plight of so many others in poorer countries in our world, I sometimes wonder how I dare to bother God with my petitions that seem so minor in comparison. Why would God be interested in whether my girls are home-educated or go to school, when so many children cannot have any education? Why would God be interested in my struggle to make ends meet, when others are starving? His gracious answers to such prayers refute this false humility. God is big enough to attend to each and every one of us. God cares about each and every one of us. The amazing reality fuels my faith for harder times ahead. It makes me feel loved, cared for and appreciated. It takes my breath away.

God's gracious generosity towards me fills me with love for Him. The rainbows in the rain assure me that nothing can separate me from the gracious Redeemer. I love Him, because He first loved me. It also makes the plight of my neighbours my problem.

Sometimes, this can seem an impossible task. I can be overwhelmed by the sheer need I am faced with. Change can seem unattainable. Situations can appear hopeless.

Problems can look as if they are irresolvable. It is then I remember people such as Efren and Jessica and believe in the miraculous transformation God can bring to the most hopeless of cases. When Jessica's mother committed suicide, and she was a frightened, lonely, grief-stricken little girl, no one imagined she would grow into the beautiful, confident young woman she is today. No one believed that her father would give up drugs, crime and drink, and be a responsible, loving father. No one supposed his ex-wife would take him back and become a loving mother to Jessica. Yet, the grace and power of God is sufficient and able to bring about these miracles in the hearts of men and women. Witnessing such manifestations of God's sovereignty enables me to believe anything is possible. They enable me to believe that God will overcome evil with good, that one day the battle between good and evil raging in our world will be won. They make me believe it is worth doing our little bit, every single day, to help a fellow human being as our contribution in that battle.

THE AUTHOR

Andrea Gardiner was born in Kent and educated at Headcorn Primary School, Underhill Preparatory School, Ashford School for Girls and Edinburgh Medical School. She pursued training as a General Practitioner in Aberdeen and Shetland before heading to Ecuador in 2005. She is founder of the Christian Charity Project Ecuador, a ministry that reaches out through healthcare, child sponsorship, building projects and a sewing project. You can read her blog at www.andysintheandes.blogspot.com.

You can find out more about the charities mentioned in this book on the following websites:

 Project Ecuador www.projectecuador.co.uk

Orphaids working with those suffering from HIV in Ecuador and Colombia www.orphaids.org

Life in Abundance Trust working with the disabled in Ecuador www.liat-ecuador.org

You can find photographs to accompany the book at: http://www.tpinterest.com/andyintheandes1/

MORE BOOKS BY ANDREA GARDINER

Guinea Pig for Breakfast
A Rich Tapestry of Tragedy, Hope and Love in Ecuador
By Andrea Gardiner
ISBN 978-1-78148-580-4

The first book in the series, this is the remarkable true story of a young British doctor who travels to humid, insect-infested Ecuador and sets up a village health centre and child sponsorship scheme. Young free and single, and dedicated to her mission, she is certainly not expecting to encounter love. Should she open her heart? Or will doing so lead to an end of all her dreams? This unforgettable account of lives touched and changed by heart breaking tragedy and restoring, redeeming love will transport you to a land brimming with iguanas and humming birds, and leave you inspired.

The Adventures of Tamarita Rachel
By Andrea Gardiner
ISBN 10-1492296783

Tamarita Rachel lives with her little sister Emily, her Mummy and her Papi among the banana plants in Ecuador. Join her as she goes on her adventures; discovering iguana eggs, visiting Indians, helping little boys go to school, and lots more. There is never a dull moment in these lively tales, which are particularly suited for 4 – 8 year olds.

"*The Adventures of Tamarita Rachel* nicely brings across not only what it's like to live in another country, but also the needs of those less fortunate than us… It would be a nice stepping stone to talk about living in another country, mission work, how we can help, and then lead into whichever missionary your church supports and how your church helps them to help the local people." Wendy Sparkes, Author

A free unit study and worksheets for children to accompany the book are available to download on www.projectecuador.co.uk.

Guinea Pig for Breakfast Recipe Book
By Andrea Gardiner
Published on Kindle

Try some mouth-watering Ecuadorian recipes from this collection of authentic dishes. Bring the flavour of Ecuador alive in your home.